WHY SCHOOLS FUMBLE

APPLYING THE END ZONE MINDSET TO SCHOOL IMPROVEMENT

DR. CATHY OWENS-OLIVER

Why Schools Fumble: Applying the End Zone Mindset to School Improvement

Copyright © 2021 by Dr. Cathy Owens-Oliver

ISBN 978-1-7369986-0-1

Requests for information should be addressed to Educational Effectiveness Group at www.edueffectiveness.com

Most of this publication is based on personal experience, educational research, and anecdotal evidence. Although the author/publisher has made every effort to ensure that the information in this book was correct at press time and while this publication is designed to provide accurate information in regard to the subject matter covered, the author/publisher assumes no responsibility for errors, inaccuracies, omissions, or any other inconsistencies herein and hereby displaying any liability to any party for any laws, damage, or disruption caused by errors or omissions, whether such errors or omissions result from negligence, accident, or any other calls. This publication is meant as a source of valuable information for the reader; however, it is not meant as a substitute or direct expert assistance.

Any trademarks, service marks, product names, or named features are assumed to be the property of their respective owners and are used only for reference. There is no implied endorsement if the author used one of these terms.

Content Reviewers: Samuel Green, Diana McIntosh
Cover Design: Martavius Mims, The Mims Group
Author Photo: Ashleigh Crawley, Still Shots Photography
Cover photo by Sergey Nivens, stock.adobe.com

All rights reserved.

CONTENTS

Acknowledgments	xi
Appreciation for my Personal Offensive Line	xiii
Foreword	xv
Preface	xvii
Introduction	xxi
Chapter One - The Quarterback Needs a Coach's Coach	1
Chapter Two - No Real Preseason	13
Chapter Three - Marginal Players	25
Chapter Four - Misreading the Defense	37
Chapter Five - Someone Dropped the Ball	53
Chapter Six - Adverse Climate Conditions	69
Chapter Seven - No One Called a Foul on the Play	83
Chapter Eight - Pass Interference	97
Chapter Nine - Completely Deflated Footballs	113
Chapter Ten - Headaches and Concussions	129
Chapter Eleven - Building the O-Line	147

About the Author	163
References	165
Footnotes	175

PRAISE FOR 'WHY SCHOOLS FUMBLE'

"As a former math teacher and national youth ministry director, I concur with Dr. Owens-Oliver's call to action. We do need strong school leadership and high-quality teaching in every classroom. Our communities must share responsibility for helping all children become scholars and leaders."
　—*Bishop J. Drew Sheard*
　Presiding Bishop, Church of God in Christ, Inc., MI

"In her book *Why Schools Fumble*, Dr. Owens-Oliver clearly lays out the challenges K-12th grade schools encounter. Her fresh perspective provides a systematic action plan to address schools shared beliefs, values, and assumptions. Her use of football analogies creates excellent imagery of how schools, school leaders and teachers should function to ensure students' academic and socio-emotional success. This is a must read for every leader and educator in this day!"
　—*Allison Jackson, Assistant Principal*
　Los Angeles Unified School District, CA

"A MUST READ! Dr. Owens-Oliver's lens on school improvement with an all-hands-on-deck approach could not have come at a better time! A necessary guidepost, as it provides an inquiry-based focus for school leaders and their teams to self-reflect and reimagine strategies that will absolutely accelerate learning and increase student achievement. This is the resource we've been looking for!"
　—*Kalisha Robinson, Senior Improvement Instructional Specialist Chief Academic Office, New York City Department of Education*

"I am so glad my friend, Dr. Cathy, has put her best thinking in writing to help educators do what she calls the "hard work and heart work" for school improvement. This great book not only clarifies what the ongoing problems are, but why they persist. The *Huddle Up* after each chapter provides strategies to help school teams change the way we serve our communities."
    —*Diana McIntosh, Principal*
    Winston Salem Forsyth County Schools, NC

"This riveting book should be lauded as required reading for any current and aspiring educator. Metaphorical in its clever use of foot-ball, the book explicates the criticality of partnership to ensure student success and the continual scoring of touchdowns and wins for teacher education majors and in the institutions of higher educa-tion that prepare them. Each chapter emphasizes viable strategies to propel students forward in their academic journeys. I anticipate hosting Dr. Owens-Oliver on our campus for an explicit discussion of this text, written for the ages!"
    —*Anthony A. Pittman, Ph.D., Professor and Dean*
    Claflin University School of Education

"Welcome to a magnificent 21st century playbook for cutting-edge, innovative approaches to school leadership, structure, and methods. Dr. Owens-Oliver has prepared a revolutionary masterpiece that examines modern-day academics using a sports analogy that brings it to life. This book is a touchdown!"
    —*Michael Payton, Math and Science Teacher*
    Chicago Public Schools, IL

"Why Schools Fumble is a simple and amazingly written guide for school success, using America's beloved game of football. Dr. Owens-Oliver has wittingly used the game to address our schools' most overlooked areas of deficiency and share effective strategies for students and teachers alike. More specifically, it reassesses the fundamental principles of student-centered learning and leadership. I believe this book is a win-win for every educator!"

—*Dr. Kimberly C. Manley, Adjunct Faculty*
North Carolina A&T State University

"Why Schools Fumble is an innovative manual to all who are interested, responsible, and/or a stakeholder in the education system of their community. The analogy of American football used to convey greater understanding of the problems and solutions is nothing short of brilliant. It provides meaningful insights into improving and enhancing the educational system in America."

—*Dr. Mark A, Ellis, Board Member, Louisiana Board of Ethics*
Baton Rouge, LA

To every student teacher, classroom teacher, school leader, college professor, youth minister, and concerned parent I've ever taught, trained, or coached, and in memory of Gregory Lockhart, an unforgettable student who, I realize in retrospect, taught me so much more than I taught him.

To J.C. Mylas, my eternal friend, who inspires me to keep writing.

ACKNOWLEDGMENTS

To my husband, Sidney Oliver, for teaching me how to play golf, a sport I find far less complicated than football.

To my sister and friends Sonia McGhee, Roberta Coleman, Thursday Rice, and
Dr. Rhonda Richetta, for the countless personal "football lessons for a dummy" you gave me by phone call and text, day and night.

APPRECIATION FOR MY PERSONAL OFFENSIVE LINE

Ms. Queen Penny, first grade,
who cultivated my desire to be a teacher.

Mrs. Barbara Barbour, second grade,
who showed me what not to do.

Mrs. Karen B. Lee, third grade,
for the multiplication race to the finish contest.

Mrs. Carolyn Page, fourth grade,
for not telling my mom I jumped out of the window.

Mrs. Susan Polumbo, fifth grade,
for often speaking to us in Spanish.

Mrs. Peggy Garnett, sixth grade,
for *the talk* when I finally got my *visitor*.

Ms. Catherine Farthing, seventh grade,
for consoling me when all my hair had to be cut short.

Mrs. Delores Love, eighth grade,
for picking me up on teacher workdays so
I could grade papers and decorate bulletin boards.

Mrs. Bonnie Gilchrist, ninth through twelfth grade
Honors English, for setting high standards for me.

Mr. William "Bill" Sutter, ninth through twelfth grade,
for introducing me to the marimba and always driving
me home safely after marching band practice.

Dr. Thomas Frye, eleventh and twelfth grade,
for creating a super fun Algebra III class *just for us*.

Mrs. Carol Pitts, twelfth grade,
for helping me apply for the *Teaching Fellows* Scholarship.

FOREWORD

I'd like to say I had a fairly good career in football; and contrary to popular belief, I understand the value of a team. This book will entail how school systems should incorporate a team concept to shore up a lot of schools' core values and missions led by teachers like Dr. Cathy. To be a successful school team, there needs to be leadership, teamwork, courage, determination, willingness and effort. It all starts with effort; and effort should be given effortlessly.

The right mindset and goals combined with guidance and execution will definitely bring about healthy dialogue with a clear path to change. I was blessed to have a mother who always believed that I was going to be something special and not every kid has that unconditional love and support. This is where Dr. Cathy along with school leaders can make a difference.

When I played, I challenged myself to be a game changer, a play maker, a difference maker and this is the exact mindset that every teacher should have. Be the difference for our future!

—*Terrell Owens*
NFL Hall of Fame Wide Receiver

FOREWORD

PREFACE

"Are kids failing school or are schools failing kids" is a question that keeps me up at night. Late one night, the title of this book, Why Schools Fumble, was divinely downloaded, and I started planning and writing. A few months later, I was in Maryland on business and stopped by the school where my good friend Dr. Richetta is the principal. She is a huge football fanatic, so I knew she'd be excited about the book. I sat down in her office and began to explain what I had been writing and how I see football as an analogy for school effectiveness. When I got to the part about teachers developing an "end-zone mindset," she stopped me mid-sentence to say: "Wait! You're not going to believe what my staff and I just put together." Then she flipped open her laptop and began to read to me her school's new core values. Great minds really do think alike! Here's her story.

When my friend, Dr. Cathy, asked me to write something for her book, I knew she wanted me to share my experience with guiding

PREFACE

my leadership team through an exercise to develop our core value statements. Our core value statements are simple, but the meanings behind them are cunningly aligned with the comparisons Dr. Cathy makes in this book between schools and football.

We have two core value statements. *Be on the purple field. Do the right thing.* Period. To put this in context, know that our core value statements are for us, the staff. They are not for our students or families. They are internal; their meaning is clear to us and they guide everything we do. In order for us to achieve our vision and mission (or make touchdowns, as Dr. Cathy would put it), we must all live by the same core values.

Fourteen years ago, when I became the principal of City Springs Elementary/Middle School in Baltimore, Maryland, I changed the school color to purple and painted everything I possibly could, purple. This was my attempt to use symbolic leadership to bring about the transformation our school needed. We adopted a new slogan: *It's not a color. It's an attitude*, then defined the City Springs attitude with eight attributes. We worked for seven years to raise the funds needed to turn our dilapidated playground into a turf football field and track. Of course, I pushed for our field not to be green. It had to be purple turf, thus the reference in our first core value statement to the "purple field."

All organizations should have a set of core values that guide how everyone thinks and behaves, but schools especially need them. I knew that for the most part my staff had shared values, and when someone did not stay it was because their values were not the same as the rest of us. But we had never taken the time to put our core values into written statements. So, we met over the summer to develop our core value statements. We looked at a list of 81 core values and identified the ones that described us. Then we had a remarkable discussion about who we are, what we care about, and what we need to do to accomplish our vision.

PREFACE

The discussion was mostly about how everything we do is for one thing, the children, and how we do our work with passion. We also emphasized that our work is too challenging for us not to support each other. We quickly moved into an analogy with football. Someone mentioned what happens in a football game when a player fumbles the ball. The other players do not stop and point their fingers at who dropped the ball. Instead, everybody tries to get the ball back, somebody, anybody, whoever is in the best position to do so, grabs that ball and runs with it. When the game is happening, everybody is on the field with one common goal, to win the game. No one is in the bleachers spectating, because we are a team, and everyone has to always be *on the purple field*.

We then talked about what happens in the locker room versus what happens when we are on the field just tryingto win. Our second core value statement came out of this discussion about how everyone on our team had to have integrity, promote equity, and be restorative when something goes wrong. It all boiled down to just doing the right thing, always. Period.

Today, my staff frequently will respond to me by saying "I'm on the purple field" when I ask them to do something above and beyond what is expected. Or, when I thank them for doing something extraordinary, they say, "I'm doing the right thing. Period." So, the football analogy works!

When we "fumble," it is usually because someone has walked off the field or has not done the right thing. They have lost their commitment to "getting every child in the end zone." In *Why Schools Fumble*, Dr. Cathy beautifully juxtaposes the passion and commitment football players and coaches have for the game, to the passion and commitment to the education of our youth that teachers and school leaders must have. Without it, we lose.

—Dr. Rhonda Richetta
Principal, City Springs Elementary/Middle School

PREFACE

INTRODUCTION

There are two things American sports lovers are absolutely crazy about: football and winning. The two go hand in hand. Don't underestimate the power of the pigskin. America loves football. The focus on Sunday afternoons and Monday nights across the country is crystal clear: get the ball into the end zone. Touchdown!

What if schools adopted this *football faith* and religiously committed to getting every child into *the end zone?* What if school leaders and teachers adopted the belief that, no matter what role a faculty member plays, or what positions she or he fills on the team, the ultimate goal is to get the ball, which is the student, into the end zone? Isn't that what matters most? Isn't that the purpose of the game, to get touchdowns?

Suppose we the public adopted this philosophy with schools. Imagine everyone in the school community, packed into the bleachers, cheering the school staff on and anxiously awaiting that big moment when the ball, the student, the graduate, is carried successfully into the end zone. While this analogy is a great way to

INTRODUCTION

reimagine American schools, it will remain simply a figment of our imagination unless we *stop fumbling the ball*.

According to The National Center for Education Statistics,[1] 56.5 million children are enrolled in kindergarten through twelfth grade, and there were approximately 3.7 million teachers in the year 2020. Simple math suggests there were approximately fifteen students per teacher. Of course, the equation is not that simple, but it supports the assumption that there are more than enough teachers out there to facilitate school-based problem solving and teach like champions. There are more than enough teachers to run the plays called by the principals in every school and get more students into the end zone. American schools need more touchdowns!

I believe teachers provide the best instruction they know how to deliver. But sadly, most of them don't get the number of touchdowns needed to win the game. What is *really* happening in our schools? We need to analyze the root cause of these problems so we may determine not only what really is happening among them but why it continues and what we can do to address it. When touchdowns are made on the field, the whole stadium erupts with cheering. Everyone in the stands celebrates the team player who got the ball safely there, even against all odds.

While we know drugs, alcohol, negative media, poverty, bad parenting and peer pressure are some reasons why many young people are on the wrong track, we also know some adults may be key *blockers* driving young people to hopelessness. Hopelessness keeps young people from pursuing destiny. Many have been told, *by adults*, their desires are not worth it, so they feel like they will never make it to the end zone. Some don't have the end zone in mind for themselves because they have not seen enough peers get there.

As educators, we must all stop and think about this. What have we said or done that has intentionally, or unintentionally, hindered a young person from getting into the end zone? Have we misled them to believe the end zone is not where they belong? Have we discouraged a young person from becoming an entrepreneur because of our own fear of failure? Are we the reason any student feels as though s/he does not matter? In what ways have we, inadvertently, deflated or defaced the football that was placed in our hands?

Who's responsible for making young people feel unloved, unliked, unworthy, unqualified and unfit? Who were they watching when they learned how to bully one another? Where are they getting the guns and drugs? Who is blocking them from getting and keeping their lives on course for greatness? All behavior is learned. Footballs don't make it into the end zone unless they are gripped tightly by the hands of someone who will leap over walls, knock down mountains and overcome every obstacle to get them there safely. Both educators and parents need a better grip.

Teachers should not be blamed for the ongoing fumbles of American education. All educators at all levels bear responsibility. Every person on the field and the sidelines has an important role to play. From the janitor to the principal to the superintendent, everyone shares responsibility for ensuring student learning and safety. While the responsibility is influenced by district and state policymakers, the focus is on the field, where the game is played. That is, at school, where almost all youth spend 180 days each year.

Not all young people are violent, disrespectful, disobedient and lawless. Not all of them are irresponsible, ungrateful and rude. Not all of them are prison-bound, nor do they have to be. Even those children who live on what we call "the rough side of the tracks" are important to society. We are responsible for them, too. Any weapon formed against them is formed against us because they are a part of us.

INTRODUCTION

"In a real sense, all life is inter-related. All men are caught in an inescapable network of mutuality, tied in a single garment of destiny. Whatever affects one directly, affects all indirectly.
I can never be what I ought to be until you are what you ought to be, and you can never be what you ought to be until I am what I ought to be... This is the inter-related structure of reality."
—Dr. Martin Luther King, Jr.

Having spent countless hours teaching, guiding and serving youth, while making a concerted effort to listen, *really listen*, to them, I have concluded that many of their inappropriate behaviors are symptoms of deeper issues hidden within. Once we stop labeling them based on their behavior and start seeking to better understand the impetus for the behavior, we can better serve them. This philosophy, of course, assumes we *want* to serve them.

If we, as parents, teachers, counselors, ministers and other concerned citizens don't first see our role as a *service* to young people—contributing to their visions, advancing their dreams, and holistically supporting their quest to accomplish the purpose for which they were created—we will never be an effective influence. Ineffective relationships only push them further away from the end zone.

We can never take possession of the football if we keep dropping it. We must get a good grip on student learning. While we run the world, manage the business and influence society, let us not forget that *our* children will someday be the adults who run, manage and influence the world. Let us not wait too late to train them to be leaders of tomorrow.

I share this philosophy so all adults, not just educators, will know what we must do to help young people succeed in making it to

INTRODUCTION

the end zone. While we have experienced many wins in the education industry, we continue to experience far too many losses. While teachers on the field are held accountable for what they do with the ball when it is in their hands, many of them question who *really* calls the plays? School leaders wonder why so many of those elected to the "sky box" of education have such a limited understanding of how challenging life is for teachers and students, both on and off the field.

This book is another one of my ongoing efforts to bring greater attention to several of the repeated *fumbles* in the education industry. I believe educators at-large know exactly what to do to solve problems in schools. Yet, I, and progressive educators everywhere, remain perplexed as to why most of us aren't empowered to do what we know works. This book is not intended to provide school leaders with all the answers. Its purpose is to clarify why the problems persist and make a clarion call for all stakeholders, who know what it takes to win, to come together and be real game changers.

There is no better time than now, post pandemic, to end the debate on why schools keep fumbling the ball and agree on what must be done to regain and maintain possession. We need to convene our best "end zone strategy" thinkers and doers and commit to whatever it takes to move schools forward. I have named this play *The E4 Principle*—everybody effectively engaged every day.

In this season, everyone in the building (and online) must understand the times in which we live and know what to do about the challenges we face. What we do in this season will determine if we win. The game is tedious, challenging, overwhelming and, sometimes, very dirty. But the clock is ticking. It's the fourth quarter! Huddle up! We need a winning game plan! We can't afford to keep fumbling the ball.

FUMBLE

A fumble occurs when a football player loses possession of the ball. It may be caused by a defensive player who tries to take the ball away from the person in possession of it. It includes dropping the ball or having the ball suddenly stripped away by the opposing team.

CHAPTER ONE
THE QUARTERBACK NEEDS A COACH'S COACH

COACHING

Professional coaching in fields other than sports is one of the fastest growing industries today. Both certified and self-made coaches are now offering support, in person and online, to help people get to wherever they think their next level is or should be. But this is not new for the education industry. Leadership coaching and instructional coaching have been available to educators for a very long time. To lead change, school leaders must be coached well and be able to coach others well.

On February 4, 2018, the headline news of SBNation.com read:[1] *Super Bowl 2018 final score for Eagles vs. Patriots: Eagles fought like hell to win their first Super Bowl.* "What a game," Senior Talent Manager Jeanna Thomas wrote, "...they left the Patriots plenty of time, but Brady fumbled... the Eagles fought hard... and Foles, a backup... did more than enough to win. Pretty much everybody counted out the underdog Eagles... but Foles absolutely held his own." Every school leader, a quarterback of sorts, wants their faculty and staff to have that same professional commitment. They must be willing to do more than enough to win. And, as the team leader and quarterback, s/he must do the same.

To be effective, school leaders, including but not limited to the principal, must model the leadership they want their staff to adopt. In this historical game, quarterback Nick Foles not only threw touchdown passes, but he ran the ball and made touchdowns himself. Head coach Doug Pederson coached and pushed him into this leadership performance. Behind every good quarterback is a good head coach. Both must demonstrate teamwork and leadership.

Leadership is not a status or a role you play because you have a title or credentials. Leadership is the substance of who you are. It's the hard work you do when everybody and nobody is looking. It includes all the personal and professional development you do behind the scenes so that you are ready to win during game time. Good leaders have integrity both on and off the field. They are honest with the person in the mirror.

Leadership is a public expression of who you are allowing yourself to be developed into and who you are intentionally, or unintentionally, influencing others to become. A key element of one's own self-development as a school leader is understanding that real leadership—authentic, difference-making leadership—is never solely about you.

It's not about you being celebrated. It's about the people you serve, the people assigned to your life and the team you lead. They need you to be different, to be better, and to do more. They need you to show them the way to effectiveness. Your leadership style, approach and goals are all about affecting change for the people on your team. They need to see you call the *right* play. They need to see you orchestrate touchdowns. More importantly, they need the coach, the principal, to be a *coachable coach*. A quarterback who is led well, will lead others well. When coached well, s/he will coach others well.

Touchdowns are made by the quarterbacks, who are school-based coaches calling the right plays, and by the wide receivers and running backs, who are effective teachers. A good coach must scan the field and create opportunities for teacher leaders to run the ball. When given the opportunity, teachers can become leaders who solve problems and serve students beyond their individual classrooms. School leaders must exemplify distributed leadership by giving teachers roles that will bring more of the best out of them. They must give teachers opportunities to grow and empower them to lead change.

Teachers, grade level chairs, department heads and curriculum coordinators all need quarterbacks who are willing to pour out all of themselves—what they have learned, accomplished and mastered and how they did it. They intentionally give others all the tools and tips that helped them get results in the classroom in an effort to help their colleagues get those same results. They need quarterbacks who are willing to lead with passion, play to win and leave it all on the field. These are often learned characteristics based on a leadership style developed over time. Those who do this well have watched others do it well. They model leadership by following leadership. Again, they coach well because they have been or are being coached well.

WHY SCHOOLS FUMBLE

> "However you want to build your team, you're going to have to build it around the quarterback." [2]
> —Doug Marrone, Jaguars Head Coach

While some school leaders are natural quarterbacks, most are coached into it. Even those who have always had passion for school leadership and those who have always demonstrated commitment to the team's ultimate goal—touchdowns—ask themselves: What impact does who I am becoming have on the lives of those who look to me for leadership? Effective coaches maintain a keen awareness of the need for more knowledge and skills so they can pass that knowledge and skillset onto their teams. When school leaders, administrators and principals become more focused and intentional about how their influence can shape the lives of both teachers and students, they expand their capacity to do something more, something different and something better for the *field* of education.

Leadership capacity is limited to one's ability to influence or reprove the life and work of team members who trust your decision-making. Sometimes school leaders really don't know what decision to make. It's unfortunate that, often, they are unwilling and insecure about sharing what they know or don't know. While the educational system is slow to reprove and/or remove ineffective teachers, it is quick to replace or reassign school leaders who make mistakes, even unknowingly. Several school leaders tell me they have neither the proper support in difficult environments nor the autonomy they need to explore potential options.

Having a good coach is vitally important for school leaders to analyze school-based problems and engage the whole school community in problem-solving. To effectively lead school change, and implement improvement initiatives with fidelity, school leaders need their own professional coaching and their own sounding board. They need an effective coach to help them develop the playbook and analyze each play from the sidelines. This allows them to be intentional and effective at calling and running the play on the field in real-time. Mainly, they need an effective coach in order to become an effective coach.

"Dungy stresses that coaches are essentially teachers.... They guide instead of goad, and that is perhaps the most instructive thing of all." Smith said, "We talked about...being a teacher instead of screaming and yelling...." "...I think as you look to young coaches coming up in the ranks, a lot of us have a picture of how a coach is supposed to be, how he is supposed to act...." [3]
—Karen Crouse, New York Times

It's a fact that some educators aren't coachable. This is because they are not willing to be coached. But those who are willing to be coached often become good coaches, equipped to lead other players on their team. Effective school leadership demands collaboration and consensus on strategies to win. We know winning is about getting the football into the end zone. The school leaders, or quarterbacks, cannot score all the touchdowns and win the game by themselves.

Coachable leaders win by selecting and leading team players in ways that garner whole-group engagement. In partnership with their coach, the school's "quarterback" is able to build a strong team that is committed to shared thinking, shared decision-making and shared outcomes. There is power in working together for a common goal. The focus of effective leadership is ensuring all other leaders on the team commit to their development, sharpen their focus and hone their skills to advance to their next level. When school leaders show teachers that they believe in them, teachers then believe in themselves.

"I'm on a team whose ownership and front office believes in me the way I believe in myself. And to me, that means a lot—knowing that I get to go to work every day and be the best me, and by myself." [4]
—*Christian McCaffrey, Running Back, Carolina Panthers*

School leaders who are coachable, and coached well, understand that every leader makes mistakes. All of us have something in our past that, if we had to do it all over again, we would do it completely differently. Maybe we wouldn't do it at all! No matter how far we go in life, or how successful we become, every now and then someone or something from our past takes *that thing* we thought was behind us and throws it in our face. Often, that somebody is *oneself!* We perseverate on things we wish we could undo rather than moving forward in the right direction with the right mindset of what must be done now and next. Perseverating on mistakes of the past holds us hostage to regret. But you know what? You live and you learn, …I'm in control of what I'm in control of, and that's being productive on the field.

We must let things go and press forward. Coachable school leaders will learn this lesson early as they realize there are many decisions to make when running a school and supervising the work of both adults and children. Most importantly, school leaders must understand their role as a coach and respect the role of their coach. They need their own non-evaluative coach who can provide them with the freedom to be honest about what they do not know. They need opportunities to work through feelings and complaints during sessions with their coach so as not to take it out on their staff. And they need a coach to help them engage various audiences: staff, students, parents, community, school boards and media. Quarterbacks who are coached well can lead well.

Was Belichick or Brady responsible for the Patriot's success? Brady, who doesn't appreciate this argument, responds.... "I can't do his job, and he can't do mine. So, the fact that you could say, 'Would I be successful without him? The same level of success?' I don't believe I would have been. But I feel the same vice versa as well. To have him allowed me to be the best I can be. I'm grateful for that..."[5]
—Charlean Williams, *Athlon Sports Pro Football Review*

HUDDLE UP!

- If you're the principal, be an effective quarterback—one who doesn't just call the plays but models the leadership you would want to follow.
- Demonstrate shared leadership by empowering your teammates. Scan the field and create opportunities for teacher leaders to run the ball. Set them up for wins and encourage them to "go for it."

- Begin with the end in mind. Determine what the end zone for academic success looks like for all your students and lead a strategy team determined to get there.
- Implement improvement initiatives with fidelity, do not start new programs without processes and protocols in place to ensure follow through.
- Get your own professional coach to help you develop the playbook and analyze each play from the sidelines.
- Focus on ensuring your vice or assistant principals are committed to their development and empowered to hone their skills and advance to their next level.
- Understand your role and limitations as a coach. Respect the role of your coach and be honest about what you do not know.

CHAPTER TWO
NO REAL PRESEASON

CRAFT in TWO
OFF-SEASON

PRESEASON

The preseason includes a series of games that are played before the official start of the regular season. These games do not count in the win-loss records of the teams playing; they are intended as practice for the regular season. The preseason is the time when teams allow prospects to play in a game to evaluate their potential. Since practices are usually slower and consist only of one's teammates, putting prospects into the game gives team officials a chance to see them perform against a true opponent at game speed. Effective teacher preparation is the preseason of the teaching career. It lays the foundation for effective teaching in the classroom.

I had the best teacher preparation experience one could ask for. I received the North Carolina Teaching Fellows scholarship for college. It included weekly teacher education seminars every semester beginning my freshman year. Truly a seminar, the weekly meeting provided an opportunity for my peers and me to discuss my learning experiences prior to college.

I learned about the communities in which my peers were reared, what shaped their perspectives on teaching quality, and what we all needed to learn and explore together. We discussed what worked for us and what did not. We reflected upon teachers we admired and who or what inspired us to pursue a teaching career. We talked about the mistakes we felt our teachers and principals made and the pitfalls we hoped to avoid in our own classrooms someday.

This meant that my immersion into teacher education took place well before my actual admission into the program. Throughout my college years, I had some prescribed courses and experiences, including summer enrichment activities related to teaching. It fostered a smoother transition into the teacher education program my junior year and helped me develop the professional skills, cultural awareness, and disposition for success as a classroom teacher.

The disposition of a teacher candidate is critical to success in the classroom. Teacher disposition includes those inherent beliefs, personal characteristics and intrinsic values that influence teachers' decision-making. Disposition is shaped by cultural exposure, family and community life, and one's desire to make a difference. Teacher education programs widely differ in their approach to identify and positively influence a potential teacher's disposition. Certainly, we can all agree it takes a special kind of person to be a teacher.

I love working with colleges of education to provide instructional coaching, professional development, and personal support and to college students pursuing teaching careers. As the K-12 classroom is vastly changing, colleges and universities (especially high minority serving institutions) need help ensuring readiness for their new teachers. Emphasis on recruiting and retaining teachers of color yields better learning for African American and Hispanic students who desperately need more teachers who look like them and can identify with their experiences.

All my life, I wanted to be a teacher. I never thought I would become a *teacher's teacher,* and I certainly never thought I would train college faculty all over the country—an accomplishment I refer to as teaching the teachers who teach the teachers. At five years old, I lined my dolls and teddy bears across the sofa to teach them. I stretched my very threatening yardstick toward each one and demanded that they recite the alphabet aloud. I did not allow my inanimate students to say, "Eleminopee," in a rush. What effective teacher would ever allow that? In my classroom, letters twelve through sixteen had to be pronounced slowly and accurately: "L, M, N, O, P."

Also included in my living room class was an incredibly special student, Mr. Potato Head. He had lots of potential, but his nose was missing. This was my first career experience teaching a student with special needs, and I did not want to let him down. I knew he would have trouble fitting in with my other students because my mother found him at a yard sale. So, he came into my class as an orphan.

At that time in my career, I had no access to professional development training in differentiating instruction or writing individualized education plans. So, I had to make it up as I went. I explained to the other students that we had a newcomer, and I was counting on them to be kind and make him feel welcome. I had the most obedient, friendly, inanimate students. They quickly embraced Mr. Potato Head. I think he fared well, even without a nose. It's funny how it never dawned on me back then how awkward it is for a teacher to refer to her student as "mister."

The mere idea of being a teacher excited me so much that I kept personal notes throughout my elementary school years of what I felt my teachers did well and not so well. The good things were things I wanted to someday replicate in my own classroom. Whatever I perceived as bad teaching practices were written as reminders of what I did not want to do or be in my future classroom.

Both the good and bad teachers I had influenced my own teacher development. At the center of my work as a teacher, teacher leader, instructional coach and education policy analyst, is my commitment to equity—equitable teaching and learning in every classroom. Growing up in a poor, rural community, I lived and learned on the downside of the equity divide. I wanted more for my students once I became a teacher. I want more for the students in classrooms today.

In some ways, all of my learning experiences have served as a preseason to the teaching profession. Certainly, my college years provided a strong foundation for me. But looking back, after more than twenty-five years in the field of education, I remain convinced that ten weeks of clinical practice in the classroom is not by any means an adequate pre-service internship.

PRESERVICE

...is a period, usually in the final year or semester of college, during which student teachers are assigned to a school to receive on-the-job training from a mentor teacher. During this pre-service or clinical experience, the student teacher practices using instructional strategies and classroom management skills while watching and working alongside the mentor. After observing the mentor, and getting to know the students, the student teacher eventually assumes full responsibility for managing the classroom and providing instruction, while the mentor observes and gives feedback for improvement.

Preseason underpins the success or potential success of a football team. This is the time when players work on mental stamina, body building, field exercises and catching the football. They work on their teamwork—learning and practicing new plays, anticipating a player's next move and building sportsmanship.

Another important aspect of a preseason is that some players get a full understanding of what it takes to win. They get an up-close idea of what will be required of them on the field. They are able to determine if they need to increase their speed or become more intuitive. They can pay more attention to what could go wrong during a play, anticipating quick changes. They also learn what to do when someone drops the ball.

As much as the preseason allows football players to prepare, it also helps them determine if they are not ready to play the game. It helps the player learn if they really don't have what it takes. It also helps them understand what role or position to play and what is expected of them in that role.

For many student teachers, the preseason is a three-month clinical experience, or internship, in the second semester of their senior year of college. This brief internship is preceded by several weeks of field observations. The student teachers visit the classrooms of licensed teachers to observe them teaching. Usually, the teacher education faculty gives reflection activities and assignments to guide what student teachers should look for during these observations.

Field observations often include sitting in on a parent meeting, attending a school staff meeting, witnessing an Individualized

Education Plan or IEP meeting (for special education), participating in a professional development session, visiting with the school counselor or principal or perhaps attending an afterschool event.

These observational experiences continue during the first few weeks of the clinical experience as the student teacher observes how the mentor teacher engages with students, meets with her/him to discuss and develop lesson plans, notes how the students respond to instruction and tries to learn students' names. After these few weeks of preparation, student teachers phase into full responsibility for teaching. In many colleges, full-time teaching occurs from late February until April. During fall semesters, it occurs in September through mid-November. This means most student teachers get up to ten weeks of full responsibility for managing a classroom, albeit with the mentor teacher on standby at all times.

Some colleges of education realize the value of more time in the classroom and, thus, offer year-long internships. This provides student teachers with the authentic opportunity to experience a full school year in the classroom. They understand the great value, necessity and benefits of an elongated experience before real-time teaching. Teacher candidates need a mix of opportunities to see all aspects of teaching during their early field experiences. They need high-quality, extensive time to practice, reflect and practice again during clinical experiences.

Without a rigorous, relevant preseason, teacher candidates don't have the opportunity to engage in deep learning about who students are, how they learn and how their varied interests, backgrounds, and experiences influence how they learn. This preseason must yield frequent opportunities to learn and run the play. The student teacher must develop the pedagogical skills and strategies that are critical to getting every student to the end zone.

Even more detrimental to the teaching profession and student learning is the *emergency licensing* phenomenon. In response to teacher shortages, many schools and districts employ teachers from other professions as *probationary* teachers and long-term substitutes. Some of them have had no real teaching experience. They have no documented results and success, and no clinical practice.

What football team has a real chance of winning when anybody can join the team as a walk-on player? They haven't had any preseason training. They haven't had any real practice on the field. They have no evidence of ever running a play, blocking a play or making a touchdown. Even worse, the player who has never played the game does not understand the rules and requirements of the game—which is a recipe for disaster.

A complete preseason experience is critical for improving teacher and student performance in the classroom. Teacher candidates need year-long opportunities to develop and practice teaching skills. The policies and processes by which teachers are licensed must be reviewed and analyzed. Licensure exams need to be critically examined by a diverse team of education experts to determine if they reflect specifically what teachers need to know and be able to do *today*, with more emphasis on how to teach than what to teach.

More attention must be paid to teacher shortage areas—why we have them and how to address them. Emergency licensing policies must be carefully reviewed and revised so that there are uniformed standards and expectations for what probationary educators are hired to do. These are the first steps to recruiting and retaining effective teachers and ensuring only qualified players are drafted into the profession. Subpar, marginal educators are detrimental to school progress.

HUDDLE UP!

- Carefully consider a teacher's disposition when choosing new staff. Look for the right fit based on

decision-making, and inherent beliefs about student learning.
- Establish a schoolwide learning community where both adults and students are willing to learn and grow.
- Promote collaboration and teamwork. Don't tolerate cliques and separatists.
- Provide school-based professional development tailored to teachers' specific needs and interests.
- Make sure new hires, especially novice teachers who are new to the profession, understand what role or position to play and what is expected of them in that role.
- Guide your staff's understanding of the needs and differences of families in your school's community.
- Make teacher's pursuit of knowledge of students' individual learning needs as well as assets a priority practice for which they are held accountable.
- Examine staff shortage areas thoughtfully, placing the right people in the right roles for which they are best qualified, even if they may be initially uncomfortable.

CHAPTER THREE
MARGINAL PLAYERS

JOURNEYMEN

...are marginal athletes with short-term contracts who travel from team to team, as back-up players. They fill in for quarterbacks or other starters. They move about as free agents, hoping a team will accept their limited skills. They are often hired as temps for injured quarterbacks. Allowing marginal school leaders and teachers to continue working, without improvement, limits student learning and lessens school effectiveness.

The New York City Department of Education has reassignment centers, known as rubber rooms, where educators charged with misconduct are held. According to state law, tenured teachers cannot be terminated without arbitration. So, millions of taxpayer dollars pay for them to spend the day in a place where they can read, relax, surf the web, sleep or do whatever else they choose. During this time of holding, they earn a full salary.

While I don't think the rubber room is a solution for teacher misconduct, I do think poor teaching is certainly a cause for reassignment to somewhere other than the classroom. But marginal teachers also get to sit and relax, just passing time in schools where principals don't have enough documented evidence to support their dismissal. Many are underqualified and contribute negatively to school culture.

In schools, both principals and teachers may be journeymen. The journey of a marginal teacher may go on and on. Because they are easy to hire and difficult to terminate, they journey from school to school. They may be good teammates to have at practice but don't have what it takes to lead. Unless they are called upon to replace a starter, they are seldom on the field during a real game. Many are good enough to get on a team, but their inconsistency and subpar performance keep them on the bench.

Often, students in high-need and low-performing schools end up with low-performing, marginal teachers. In 2007, researchers found that "poor, minority and low-performing students are much more likely to have teachers who are inexperienced, uncertified and less academically able than their higher-performing peers."[1]

Later in 2016, a study of equity gaps found that high poverty, minority students are more likely to be taught by unqualified teachers in 25 of 38 states.[2] Since then, the problems have persisted. Students with greater need are more often taught by low-performing teachers.

The teaching profession is one of high stress and limited pay. Obviously, teachers want to be in the best schools, with access to quality resources and supportive communities. More experienced, or even burned-out teachers, often seek *easier* job placements because they feel they've earned it. They often get recruited and hired at schools with better working conditions, better technology and newer buildings. They don't want to teach in high-poverty communities facing extreme lack.

Some people say, "What you don't know can't hurt you." But what students don't know, or don't learn, absolutely will hurt them. But the fact that they *don't* know doesn't mean they *can't* know. A good education is critical. They can't get a good education without good teachers. It is not enough to *say* all children can learn; we must put proper measures in place to ensure they *do* learn.

One proper measure is ensuring students are taught by effective teachers. I use the term *effective* because the political system created its own criteria for *highly qualified* status, which has more to do with credentials based on licensure exam scores than proven practices and student learning outcomes. The distribution of teachers with varied credentials makes a significant difference in student learning. When high need students are placed with teachers who lack proper qualifications, the equity gap widens.

One key aspect of effective teaching is knowing the students—how they think, how they learn, what their family traditions are and what values shape the way they interact with others. Often, marginal teachers don't have this knowledge and don't know how to acquire it. Knowing something about students' families, their interests, and their attitudes about life and learning enable teachers to provide tailored instruction and more engaging educational experiences.

Historically, teachers have not been taught essential skills and content necessary for reaching children from various cultural backgrounds. Instead, they have been taught to effectuate mainstream culture. White teachers teach the way they've been taught, largely based on their personal cultural exposure and beliefs. They are allowed to be marginal teachers as it relates to culturally responsive pedagogy. They fare well because they don't have to learn *whiteness* (as do teachers of color) and they aren't expected to learn *blackness* or unlearn *whiteness* in order to be a teacher. But culturally relevant curriculum and differentiated teaching methods are key components of instructional quality and student success.

Placing weaker teachers with students who live in high-poverty communities exacerbates the equity gaps caused by their socioeconomic conditions. Students in schools with ineffective teachers and inadequate materials have inefficient learning experiences. Many school districts are often forced to accept marginal players, journeymen or mere "warm bodies" who can "cover" classrooms but may not be fully credentialed to yield maximum learning results for students.

In 2009, researchers surveyed 15,000 teachers and 1,300 administrators and found that more than 80 percent of administrators and almost 60 percent of teachers reported there was a tenured teacher in their school who delivers poor instruction. They also found that 75 percent of the teachers were not given recommendations on how to improve their teaching skills. In five years, 50 percent of the districts included in the study had not terminated a low-performing, or *marginal* teacher.[3]

In 2017, Matthew Kraft of Brown University and Alison Gilmour of Vanderbilt University, released a follow up study examining data from 24 states that had revised and supposedly improved their systems for evaluating teacher effectiveness. They reported that several principals felt:

- It is not fair to rate teachers as below proficient without

being able to provide the support they need for improvement.
- Giving a low rating to potentially good teachers could be counterproductive to their development.
- Delivering the message of low performance is a difficult conversation not all principals are capable of leading; and
- First-year principals don't want to watch a teacher walk out the door feeling dejected because s/he lost the job.[4]

Is it fair to teachers and their students if the school principal cannot help underperforming teachers improve their practice? If an ineffective teacher has potential that hasn't been reached, how long must students receive limited instruction while the teacher develops skills? If principals find it difficult to have conversations with ineffective teachers about their performance, how long should the conversations be tabled for principals to become more comfortable? Who suffers when low-performing teachers are allowed to continue working so the principals won't feel bad about firing them? This is a travesty.

During the off-season, Patriots Head Coach Bill Belichick intentionally selected athletes who were not the highest draft picks. But he saw greatness in them that had not been cultivated yet. Even without the higher draft players, he and Tom Brady transformed the Patriots and led them to six Super Bowl wins.[5] He as a senior coach, and Brady as a junior coach, worked together with the promising athletes to expand their skills.

This is how leaders build team capacity and pull out of people a higher quality performance. This is what was amazing about Brady's move from the Patriots to the Buccaneers. During Super Bowl LV, it was evident how hard he and all other team leaders had worked to teach and train the team, stretch their individual skills, influence their confidence and push them to a level of excellence they didn't know they could reach.

Perhaps school districts need to adopt the Brady-Belichick strategy for increasing the effectiveness of staff who have potential but aren't meeting it. Why aren't marginal teachers inspired and admonished to build their skills? Content coaches and professional development experts must be put in place to further the learning and improve the classroom practice of marginal teachers—especially those who really want to do better and may not know where to start.

"The single most important thing in a child's performance is the quality of the teacher."
—Michael Gove, Former Education Secretary, United Kingdom

Marginal performance is another reason why teacher licensing may need to be restructured so that hiring of teachers is not largely based on test scores. It is impossible for every player on every football team to know every play of every other team. Even though they are all football players, there are some plays, relevant to a certain team that must be learned once the player joins that team. The primary focus is that those on the field understand how to play football and what to do when the ball is in their hands. Learning how to run a play is secondary to learning to how to play the game.

Regarding teacher licensure and preparation, the emphasis should not be on how much content teachers know but the extent of their ability to teach that content in a variety of ways to a varied group of student learners. The focus cannot be solely on content, as it is changing and expanding daily. The math in a fourth-grade class today is quite different than it was years ago. But knowing how to teach it is what's most important for classroom readiness. It's time for the education industry to seriously rethink what the key performance indicators are for teachers.

When I was a new English teacher, I did not know all literature and had not read everything on the districtwide reading list. But I knew the methods for how to teach various curriculum and how to connect it to student interests and learning styles. That which I had not read, I was able to read before assigning it to my students. Many new teachers, and almost all marginal ones, have not learned key teaching strategies and their value. Marginal, underqualified teachers who have not had training in how to implement culturally responsive pedagogy, as well as other strategies for student engagement, are unable to get students into the end zone for touchdowns.

So, these questions remain on the table. Are students failing school or are schools failing students? When a student fails, is it solely the student's fault? When students perform marginally, after an entire school year with an assigned teacher, is the student the problem? When a student who was struggling to read in fourth grade has that same struggle in eighth grade, is it because s/he did not try hard enough? After four years, whose marginal performances demand closer scrutiny—that of the students or the teachers?

HUDDLE UP!

- Don't tolerate poor teaching. Recognize it, call it out, and help underperforming teachers improve their practice.
- Provide opportunities for all teachers to learn and observe other effective teachers.
- A journeyman's reputation matters. Find out why your journeyman consistently moves from school to school and ensure you have him or her in the right role (with

appropriate professional support and instructional coaching).
- Recognize and value potential because teachers who want to be better will often "out serve" those who think they are the best.
- Place higher need students with higher performing teachers.
- Be intentional about finding teachers of color.

CHAPTER FOUR
MISREADING THE DEFENSE

MISREADING THE DEFENSE

During the huddle, the quarterback calls an offensive play. Sometimes, when he gets to the line of scrimmage, he sees the defense has changed formation, so he calls an audible change of play. If he misreads the defensive line data and calls the wrong play, he could inadvertently throw an interception. A quick analysis of the defensive formation gives him information he can use to make split-second decisions in the pocket, hoping it's the right call. Student performance data, including but not limited to test scores, must be properly interpreted by school leaders so they can determine the right short or long-term strategy for improvement.

When a quarterback decides to change the play, on the spot, because of what he sees the defense do, it's a risky decision. If he misreads the offense and deviates from the play that was originally decided upon, the misread could result in an interception. He may call an audible play based upon the data he scanned and later realize, after looking at the outcome, it was the wrong call.

Quarterback Peyton Manning, who played for the Indianapolis Colts and the Denver Broncos, was known for making split-second decisions in the pocket. When linemen saw him pointing down the field and yelling the audible call, "Omaha," they knew he wanted them to go to Plan B. Manning became widely known for making split-second decisions in the pocket, calling a strategic last-minute change of play.

Examples of audible calls in the education industry may include dividing two classes of third graders, such that one teacher focuses on science and math while the other teaches only reading and social studies. Having the students "change classes" this way, mid-year, plays to the strengths of the two teachers and increases student learning outcomes.

Another example of an audible is the misdiagnosis of students with special needs and class placements based on test-taker data. A struggling first grader may be assumed as intellectually disabled. But if s/he missed several days of school in kindergarten due to negligent parents, the issue is not inability to learn; it's lack of exposure to information and effective teaching as well as lack of substantial data to support intellectual deficiency.

Additional evidence of the fact that many students are labeled wrong and not taught effectively is the achievement gap. This gap in achievement, as well as equity, means there is great disparity between the academic performance of students of color and their White counterparts. Perpetuated by ineffective (or marginal) teachers, it shows up in the grades students receive in school, the rates at which they graduate from high school, their college course loads, college grade point averages and, of course, their scores on standardized tests. This is an equity issue.

One of the reasons why the gap persists is because many students of color are not prepared for kindergarten. This is why several states now mandate that four-year-old children attend pre-school. Many states also provide assistance to ensure parents can afford to send their children to pre-school. Research shows that the fastest brain growth is from birth to age five. Any lag in the first three years usually yields no recovery. They will always fall behind in learning. The gap begins as early as nine months old and can last for two years. By fifth grade, most Black males are two years behind (Iruka, 2016).[1]

Sara Neufeld highlighted, "President Obama has reignited... early childhood education by proposing universal preschool for four-year-olds from low- and moderate-income families. But with much of a child's brain development occurring in the first three years of life, advocates say even that is too late.... Poor babies as young as nine months show a gap in cognitive development compared with wealthier peers, a gap that triples by the time they are two years old."[2]

We all take tests. We take a test to get a driver's license, a job or even a clean bill of health. Educational testing is not going away. Policymakers in the educational system see testing as an important way to measure student progress and evaluate teacher performance. The question is: Why does there continue to be such a huge difference in test scores by race?

STANDARDIZED TESTS

...are assessments comprised of the exact same test questions, testing time, and scoring processes for all students. Testing companies assert that this level of standardization makes it easy for educators and policymakers to compare test-taker performances against national standards, then determine the progress or lack of progress for students, teachers, and schools. Test data is also used to determine norms, including that of race and gender.

Who determines what the standard should be? The national emphasis on a common set of core curriculum standards was intended to align curriculum across state lines and ensure a higher quality education for all students, no matter where they live and go to school. But there remains concern that common curriculum for everyone pushes teachers to focus on preparing students for "the test" only.

Often teaching is directed toward improving student scores on tests and not ensuring that they fully comprehend information and can apply it to life experiences. Some argue that increased emphasis on passing tests perpetuates lack of emphasis on critical thinking. Students are pushed to find that one right answer, as if there aren't multiple answers and possible solutions.

Perhaps the issue is not the test in and of itself as much as how the test results are used. They should be used for diagnosis rather than prognosis. Tests should be used to "diagnose" what students' strengths and challenges are as learners. Testing should not be used to create a label or a prognosis, based on perceived weaknesses in learning. A diagnostic test is an evaluation of "what is happening now" and assesses what a learner does or does not know. But a prognosis is a prediction of "what is most likely to happen next" and should inform instructional planning.

So often, children are labeled negatively because they did not score well on a test. But test results should help teachers determine what children's strengths and weaknesses are. Teachers should use the test results to determine what the students don't understand and what material they haven't yet mastered so they can teach the information in ways students will better understand.

In his book, scholar Alfie Kohn writes, "Test scores result in blaming students for what they don't know... As the primary criteria for judging children, teachers and schools—indeed as the basis for flunking students or denying them a diploma... Tests have become a mechanism by which public officials can impose their will on schools..."[3]

In a state-sponsored meeting in Maryland, teachers gathered to express their discontentment with standardized tests. One teacher said, "They don't provide any meaningful feedback for teachers." Another complained that her "students working on the new tests repeatedly answered: "I don't know, I don't know, I don't know." [4]

There is something wrong about testing someone on information they haven't yet been taught. A mother would never test a two-year old on how to tie his or her shoes, ride a bike or bake a cake. She knows the child does not have that knowledge yet. Young people need ample time to study and prepare for tests. Preparation must include effective study skills, as well.

Educators do want students to get into the academic end zone and be well-prepared for the future because employers want them to be professionally trained to do a job successfully. Alfie Kohn also wrote, "How many jobs demand the employees come up with the right answer on the spot, from memory, while the clock is ticking? ... And when someone is going to judge the quality of your work, whether you are a sculptor, a lifeguard, a financial analyst, a professor, a housekeeper, a refrigerator repairman, a reporter, or a therapist, how common is it for you to be given a secret pencil-and-paper exam? Isn't it far more likely that the evaluator will look at examples of what you've already done, or perhaps watch you perform your normal tasks?"[5]

The Scholastic Aptitude Test (SAT),[6] first administered in 1926, is a standardized test most students are required to take before college admission. It is the revision of an IQ test created in the 1901 French War as a recruitment tool. The test was not designed to determine what specific content students need to know to perform well in a certain field.

It was originally designed to determine if young White males had enough "innate mental ability" to receive a scholarship to highly competitive Ivy League Schools such as Harvard, Princeton, and Yale. But by the 1940s, the SAT became the primary admissions requirement for colleges across the United States.

In 1975, the Federal Trade Commission (FTC) investigated[7] the extent to which the SAT yields an "uncoachable" aptitude and whether students could improve their scores. Their 1978 report opens with: "Schools claimed that their programs could help students improve their scores... However, the Educational Testing Service maintained the coaching will do little help." This continues to be a debate as educators grapple with whether the test is biased, irrelevant, and unnecessary.

In the 1990s, some twenty years later, the SAT was finally changed to include more reading comprehension and mathematics. In 2001, there was support for dropping the SAT because of its deemed irrelevance to what students actually learn during school. In 2005, the test was changed again to include essay writing and more rigor. It's strange how we think more rigor and difficulty of tests will increase students' content knowledge.

According to the College Board's 2017 annual report,[8] almost two million students took the SAT and only half of them passed. On their website, the organization describes its work as "helping millions of students navigate the transition to college through programs like the SAT." In 2020, they reported more than two million students took the test, but average scores were down nine points and less than half of the test-takers met or exceeded the college readiness standard.[9]

Why is an 85-year-old test designed to assess the I.Q. of military recruits, despite its redesigns, still in use today as one of the leading college admission requirements for all students? Why is this test still relevant when aptitude is limited to exposure? You can't know or recall information to which you have never been exposed. How do you study when you don't have clear information about what to study? Is the objective to learn well or guess well?

Perhaps, if you don't do well on an aptitude test, it's because you cannot relate, or you haven't been exposed to the material. If you have not been exposed or introduced to certain information, why would someone hold you accountable for it? Do these tests of broad, random facts and ideas inadequately prepare students for college? Given the nature of the test questions, and the backgrounds of the people who write the questions (or items), could there be a bias against certain test-takers?

The inordinate pressure to pass these tests is evidenced by the recent *Operation Varsity*[10] scandal wherein the FBI discovered celebrities Lori Loughlin and Felicity Huffman were among fifty parents who paid millions of dollars to bribe their children's way into elite universities. This included paying people to take the SAT for their children, paying for unlimited time extensions to complete the test, and possibly bribing test administrators and proctors. This led to the decision made by several Ivy League schools to eliminate the SAT requirement indefinitely.

Not only has the pressure to pass these tests had a negative impact on students, but also on teachers, well-prepared teachers, who struggle to pass the standardized teacher licensure exams.

During the pandemic, various state education leaders relaxed testing requirements to give teachers who successfully complete educator preparation programs entry to the profession.

Given the teacher shortage, why isn't anyone asking what would happen if teacher licensure exams were eliminated altogether and education leaders simply trusted that four years in college, several months observing classrooms and practicing teaching are a better indicator of teacher readiness than guessing at a sampling of questions from broad content that is ever expanding? Some states have elected to suspend teacher licensure testing requirements. It will be interesting to learn, in the absence of these tests, whether teachers are unprepared for the classroom. How will teachers be licensed for the global classroom in the "edtech" world?

Children are exposed to new information when they read, travel, and explore new ideas and concepts. If they live and learn in an area that does not foster this kind of exposure, their intellectual content is limited, regardless of their intellectual capacity. The bigger question is how do these tests relate to the basic or experiential knowledge and skills demanded by various professions students may pursue? What about students who do not do well on the SAT, but may perform well regarding everything else—including end-of-course grades, behavior, community service, public speaking and writing, technology and design?

William Ayers wrote: "Standardized tests can't measure initiative, creativity, imagination, conceptual thinking, curiosity, effort, irony, judgment, commitment, nuance, good will, ethical reflection, or a host of other valuable dispositions and attributes. What they can measure and count are isolated skills, specific tasks and functions, the least interesting and least significant aspects of learning."[11] What will testing look like in the global classroom?

Overemphasis on testing has created a two-way crisis in America. On one hand, misuse of test results has caused many students to be mislabeled, misunderstood and miseducated. It has also caused them to miss opportunities. On the other hand, it has caused teachers to dumb down the curriculum. This limits students from engaging in critical thinking, life application of the content learned, and more hands-on learning activities. Teachers may teach primarily based on information covered on tests, which pushes out students who may not be good test-takers.

Researchers found that standardized tests like the SAT make Black students extremely nervous because, "they fear incorrect answers will confirm negative stereotypes about their race."[12] So, both the achievement gap and the standardized tests that perpetuate it are a means of pushing them down and out of the public education system—one that was never designed with them in mind.

Leading antiracist scholar Ibram Kendi writes: "Standardized tests have become the most effective racist weapon ever devised to objectively degrade Black minds and legally exclude their bodies." He asserts that to believe in the achievement gap is to believe in a racial hierarchy "constructed by our religious faith in standardized testing."[13]

Perhaps he's right. Do we worship these test results? Do we bow down to the testing industry? Has the testing industry become a Pharoah? Is it the education god to whom we all must pay homage and financial offerings? Have you Googled the startling stories about all the young people who committed suicide after receiving their test scores? What a real sacrifice parents and children make to score well on these standardized tests.

State and district school leaders and policymakers perseverate over test-taker performance. Teachers have been caught and arrested for changing students' answers to get better test results for themselves, not for the students, so they can keep their jobs. Parents have been imprisoned for bribery and cheating on these high-stake tests. Some did this without telling their children so they could protect them from any shame and anxiety of not passing. The careers and character of so many adults have crumbled under the weight of standardized testing, while many question who set "this standard" in the first place.

Kendi says people in America, "Have been led to believe that intelligence is like body weight, and the different intellectual levels of different people can be measured on a single, standardized weight scale. Our faith in standardized tests causes us to believe that the racial gap in test scores means something is wrong with the Black test takers—and not the tests.[14]

Interpretation and application of student test data is often misread, just as a quarterback may misread or misinterpret data he gets from defensive formation. When a quarterback calls an audible play based on what move he assumes the defensive line will make, his play may be successful. But there's a chance it may be detrimental because data is often skewed and misleading.

How we label schools and students as failing is often based on a misread. Schools often use test-taker performance data to determine a student's level of need or disability. This may lead to mislabeling of student exceptionalities. Data easily can be misinterpreted, given a host of varied circumstances and intentions.

How schools and state boards of education address the assessment conundrum, as a result of a national pandemic, will be critical to what schooling (full time and in person) will look like. How do we assess student learning in the future? Surely, we don't expect to get accurate data from the usual standardized tests. What kind of feedback on individual student learning will teachers produce? What, if anything, will substantiate traditional grading methods?

We must teach higher order thinking skills. The ability to think critically and make good decisions is central to student learning both at home and at school. Both parents and teachers are key influencers in students' ability to engage in problem-solving, fact-finding and synthesis of ideas. When students are not taught to think critically, outcomes on traditional tests may have limited value.

The need for redesigning grading practices and protocols is greater now than ever. Relying on traditional scoring methods spurs the likelihood of misreading testing results. This can lead to

school leaders and policymakers calling more wrong plays and causing teachers to fumble the ball.

Stanford University's professors examined 47 years of test data from 98 tests of reading, math, and science for almost three million teenage test-takers. In their report, they found that this *opportunity gap*, based on the relationship between student achievement on tests and socioeconomic status, neither has grown nor closed since 1966.[15] If this data is accurate, it suggests that any improvement in teacher education, increase in school-based professional development in math and science, statewide emphasis on literacy and STEM, leadership coaching for principals, and culturally competent instruction has had absolutely no significant impact on improving student learning. Can this be true?

In a conversation with civil rights leader and national consultant, Dr. Terrence Roberts of the *Little Rock Nine*—one of the most poignant stories of Black history—I asked him if he agrees that we've come a long way in American education and how so? His striking response was, "No, not when it comes to education." He went on to explain how issues of access and equity continue to be unaddressed. He told me he questions if America *really* wants everybody to be educated because if we did, we would not spend more money on weapons than schooling. I was fascinated by all the solutions he shared in that conversation and saddened that we, as a country, have yet to apply them.

HUDDLE UP!

- Beware of misdiagnosis of students with special needs and wrong placements based on test-taker data. Ensure special education staff and core teachers work collaboratively.
- Use test performance data to diagnose student needs for more prescriptive instruction and tutoring rather than a final say on their intellectual capacity and academic future.
- Demand rigor and excellence, especially in the early grades. If you have or can get the funds and access, provide preschool, afterschool, summer school and/or any remediation and enrichment students may need.
- Include life skills, health and wellness, financial literacy, and the arts in the curriculum as opposed to solely focusing on end-of-grade testing.
- Provide opportunities for teachers to learn and employ strategies to support multiple intelligences and provide students with project-based learning opportunities. Provide training that shows teachers how to engage students in problem-solving, fact-finding, and synthesis of ideas.

CHAPTER FIVE
SOMEONE DROPPED THE BALL

DROPPING THE BALL

Each player must develop ball security skills and be able to maintain possession of it. Ball security is the ability of a player to hold on to the football during a play, no matter how tough it gets, to avoid a fumble. A player may lose possession of the football when it is knocked out of his or hands as well as when s/he drops the ball before being downed. Unfortunately, many children have been dropped by someone at home and/or at school. This trauma of being dropped or abandoned, hinders student engagement in the classroom.

When I was young, my parents separated. It was a slow, grueling process by which my dad's visits became fewer and farther between. I was six years old when I fully understood he was not coming back. Somehow, I never perceived it as though he was leaving my mother. So, I carried the painful acceptance of the fact that he was leaving *me*. I felt I wasn't good enough, smart enough, or loveable enough to make him stay with me, despite his feelings about my mother. Unfortunately, no one explained a different perspective to me.

As an adult, I realize he could have maintained a quality relationship with me outside of being with my mother, but he chose to abandon me, too. I remember overhearing countless phone conversations between them.

"What about her birthday?" Mama asked him.
"Yeah, but you already missed Christmas," she persisted.
"But I told you she really needs braces!" she yelled.
I was standing in the doorway when he drove away.
"There goes all my love," I told my mother.
"Why would you say that?" she retorted.
"He is not coming back," I muttered and walked away.

I was sad for several days after that. There is an ache inside when you know you've been abandoned. Even though my dad occasionally called, occasionally sent a card and money, and popped in for a weekend visit once or twice a year, I was never the same. Once I learned as a teenager that he married another woman who had five children, I was devastated. How could you abandon your one, flesh-and-blood daughter to raise five of someone else's children?

The domino effect of abandonment included my mother having to work three jobs. So, she wasn't at home to see me off to school. She was at work. When I came home from school, she was at work. When I played basketball, marched with the band, performed at choral and dance recitals, and suffered a devastating spelling bee loss, she was at work. She was *always* at work and, when she was at home, she was tired. Of course, my dad was *always* somewhere else. My parents dropped the ball.

"Committed and responsible fathering during a child's infancy contributes to emotional security, curiosity,
and math and verbal *skills."*
—*Vivian Gadsden, National Center on Fathers and Families*[1]

I used to think "absent father" was a term describing the deadbeat dad who refused to pay child support and had no relationship with his children. But I've come to realize that any parent, not just a father, who is not fully present in his or her child's life is guilty of abandonment—a domestic crime. I call it a domestic crime because of the traumatic damage parental absenteeism has on children's individual lives and families.

Many parents are at home, but not *present*. To be fully present is to be fully involved and aware of what's happening in children's lives. The stress of life, work, finance and personal issues, which may result in poor decision-making by parents, has a direct impact on the social, emotional, and academic development of children of all ages.

In the movie, *War Room*, both parents were at home, but their focus was elsewhere. In one scene, the mother overheard her daughter tell a friend how much she wished she lived at her house rather than at her own because her parents were always fighting. Later when the mother asked her daughter if she knew her parents loved her, the daughter responded, "Somewhat." When the mother probed to see why she felt this way, the daughter answered in tears with the following interrogation, "What's my team's name? What are our colors? What jump rope trick did I just learn to do? Who's my new coach? What award did I win last week on my team?" Sadly, and to her own surprise, the mother could not answer any of the questions accurately.[2] She had long lost possession of the ball.

Perhaps, you're with your children all day, every day. But when you are with them, are you really *with* them? When you are at home, are you really *at home*? Are you really at the game, at the birthday party, at the recital? Or are you there physically and somewhere else mentally? Are you always at work? Are you on the phone? Today, it seems everybody is always on the phone. If parents aren't careful, social media won't be the reason you've abandoned them. It will be the reason they've abandoned you.

When children are abandoned by the people responsible for them, they have no choice but to find their own way. They make choices without being informed, and they figure life out as they go rather than through the appropriate guided practice. Guided practice should come from someone they can trust, look up to and follow —someone whom they are convinced has their best interest at heart, someone fully present in their lives.

Young people know when they are being accounted for, but not cared for. They know when they are being tolerated rather than celebrated. It's not enough for parents to keep a roof over their children's heads. They must also be fully involved and aware of the day-to-day concerns, issues and activities in their children's lives, especially their thoughts. There are some very lonely children who live in households with their siblings and parents; yet, they have no real sense of family. Their parents have dropped the ball.

The foster parents of Nikolas Cruz said in an interview after the massive shooting at Parkland High School in Broward County, "We had this monster living under our roof and we didn't know. We didn't see this side of him... Everything everybody seems to know, we didn't know."[3] It saddens me that these parents were unaware of what Nikolas was thinking and feeling. Were there no small clues? In April 2019, *The Washington Post*[4] reported Cruz has been writing letters from prison to a woman suggesting they get married and name their children after guns.

When I heard stories in the news about teenage boys who had spent weeks planning online how they would shoot and kill several classmates at Columbine High School, I questioned where the parents were during this "planning" time? Did these teens feel valued? Were they unnoticed? What relationship did they have with their families and friends? What trauma had they experienced during early childhood? Was there any indication of being troubled that their teachers missed?

When I think about the shooters at Sandy Hook Elementary School, Virginia Tech and Emanuel African Methodist Episcopal Church, I wonder if their parents were fully present at home. What prevented them from being deeply involved in their children's spiritual, emotional and psychological development, as well as their goals and dreams? How did they lose possession of the ball?

I don't mean to blame parents as though they, alone, are responsible for all of their children's actions. But they are the first, and should be the most effective, influencers in their children's lives and whereabouts—not just where they are in terms of location, but where they are in their thinking. Do you know where your child is right now? Do you know where his or her head is right now? What is your child thinking about?

One of my favorite passages of Hebrew literature explains the story of a child named Mephibosheth, who was the grandson of a king.[5] During a war, his family had to run for their lives. While running, his caretaker dropped him and somehow, perhaps due to a spinal injury from being trampled, Mephibosheth was unable to walk again.

WHY SCHOOLS FUMBLE

Both his father and grandfather were killed in that war. In modern society, he would have been in kindergarten at the age of this trauma. What is the role and response of the parent, principal, teacher, school counselor and the community when a five-year-old must face both physical and emotional paralysis? Despite various entitlements he deserved as an heir of a king, Mephibosheth's whole life was tainted by this handicap.

Although the trauma resulted from an unintentional mishap by someone to whom his parents had entrusted him, he still was dropped. There are many reasons why a ball gets dropped during a football game. A player may be tackled and drop the ball. He may catch the ball but not have a good grip, causing the ball to slip through his hands. He could run the wrong route and be in the wrong place to catch the ball, so the ball drops out of bounds.

Losing possession of the ball could put a team at risk of losing the game. An important part of training includes consistent practice throwing, catching, and running with the ball. The inability to catch a pass is a clear justification of why someone is unfit for the team. Equally inept is someone who is able to catch the ball but unable to hold onto it.

Issues of abandonment, neglect and other traumas have lasting effects on a child's life, behavior and performance as a learner. These matters must be taken into consideration when planning lessons for children. Teachers and support staff must be aware of and responsive to students' varied needs and lived experiences for them to learn well.

The most valuable players (MVPs) on school teams may include the school secretary that every student and parent loves or the custodian who sings in the hallways, never forgets a birthday, and occasionally slips a few dollars to cover a student's lunch. Sometimes it's that bus driver who drives a group to school, does double duty as a teacher assistant, keeps order in the cafeteria during lunchtime, drives the basketball team to an away game, and takes great pride in being the most rambunctious fan in the bleachers.

These people are first to get to school and last to leave. They are intentional about learning students' names and making sure students know theirs. They privately give a wayward student a very stern "you better not do *that* again" directive. And the student listens.

These MVPs bring care packages to students who don't have deodorant and toothpaste. As quiet as it is kept, these people have picked a student up for school or dropped them off at home when they missed the bus. They have taken groceries to the home of *that student*, paid for *that student* to get a haircut, given *that student* a clean shirt, and even put a new tire on *that student's* car. At one time, I was *that* student and as a high school teacher, I was one of *these people,* making sure every student feels included. Today we know this as responding to the human condition, designing asset-based instruction, and honoring students' lived experiences, including being dropped.

After many years as an educator, I know so many stories of youth who have been or felt abandoned. I can categorize their stories into what I see as the four main areas or forms of abandonment:

1. Lack of adequate provision
2. Lack of emotional support
3. Lack of protection
4. Lack of discipline

The trauma of abandonment influenced my low self-esteem, attitude toward the future and perspective on relationships. I thought that when you *love less,* you *hurt less.* At an incredibly young age, abandonment crippled my ability to love and be loved.

When children are abandoned, especially girls, they internalize their own fabricated reasons why they *deserve* it. As they move through various relationships, that little abandoned girl inside reminds them in every relationship, "You are not worthy to be loved. Don't get too comfortable. This person will leave you because something is wrong with you. You're not good enough, not valuable enough. You're not worth it."

In an episode of *Oprah's Masterclass,* comedian and television personality Steve Harvey retells a conversation with his eldest son, whom he had taken to the Apollo Theater. He said his son was deeply overwhelmed to be at the theater with him, after having spent so many years, in Steve's absence, sitting up late and watching him on television performing there. Steve's opportunity with the theatre boosted his career and put him in position to take better care of his son.[6]

Even though his son acknowledged that he understood Steve's intentions, Steve says he knew, while far away trying to make a living to take better care of his son, he missed time with him. Toward the end of the episode, he explained he spent many years trying to make up for lost time. He became very intentional and dedicated to his relationship with his son and the rest of his children.

Both boys and girls who have been abandoned tend to fight—for their place or their turn. They are trying to prove that they don't need anyone and that they can make it on their own. So, how many girls and boys silently suffer after molestation, and other forms of abuse, because they don't want the abuser to leave them or cause someone else to leave them?

Even for those youth who may experience a parent dying, part of the long-term grief is not just sudden loss. It's also dealing with the fact that, intentionally or unintentionally, Mommy or Daddy left them. Abandonment is indeed a weapon, a negative force used to destroy the relationships and rapport we should have with young people. No one wants to be abandoned. Abandonment leads to stress and anxiety, which manifests itself in various ways.

Teacher education programs need to include trauma-based curricula, so teachers know how students' traumatic family issues affect learning. Beyond college, teachers need ongoing professional development training about how to recognize and respond to students' emotional trauma. School staff can't just disregard a student whose family dropped the ball. They must focus less on *why* this happened and *how to address it*. They need to build a rapport with students, understand their feelings, and experiences to offer appropriate services and support.

"As a high school basketball and football coach, I believe if you show students you love them and care about their success beyond the game, they will work hard on and off the field. When you build meaningful relationships with them and their families, it makes an impact on the whole community."
—*Elder Charles H. Thomas, Sr.*
Western Branch High School, Chesapeake, VA

When we hear, "It takes a village to raise a child," we must stop seeing that as solely a famous African proverb. Instead, we must see it as the mantra for how schools can be successful in educating *all* children. The school and its surrounding community *are* the village. To be effective, teachers must see themselves as part of the village. They must see themselves as key players on the football team, relentlessly dedicated to the team's ultimate goal: getting the ball in the academic end zone.

Everyone in a community must get involved in the educational advancement of its youth. There must be community-based programs to ensure that students do well in school. The local community must be the resource young people can turn to for not only food and assistance, but help finding jobs, getting an education, developing parenting skills and dealing with trauma.

Children spend approximately 180 days a year in school and 185 elsewhere. The educational system alone cannot solve all the problems of our communities. Students and teachers need outside support. Community leaders and faith-based organizations must see education as equally important as other facets of outreach ministry.

"Improving schools and increasing learning is the responsibility of everyone. Churches must get involved in supporting schools in their local community. Children belong to God and we all have a part to play in shepherding their personal and academic development."
—*Bishop Charles E. Blake, Sr.*
West Angeles Church of God in Christ

What can you do for the children in your community?

First, you must understand the students in your sphere of influence. Figure out their needs as learners and determine what you and other adult members of your community can do to address those needs. It is not okay for community leaders to be completely oblivious to who young people are and the challenges they face locally. We can't just *hope and pray* that they do well in school, graduate, get good jobs, and live well. We have to develop programs and implement strategies to *ensure* they do. Students in your community should have every opportunity to be successful in the classroom.

Why can't your local community be an environment where knowledge and understanding of reading, writing and math is made age-appropriate and readily available to every child who wants it? Miseducation is already happening in public schools. Students don't need to get it at home, too. This does not necessarily mean your neighborhood needs to start its own school. Start by convening with the educators in your community and developing afterschool, Saturday school and summer school programs that will advance the learning of those students with a learning lag.

Celebrate the teachers in your community. They, too, are on the front lines. Be kind to them and say, "Thank you." Support their classrooms. Donate resources and materials. Show your appreciation for the sacrifices they make. Show up for them and cheer them on the way you would for a football team.

Contact your local political representatives and advocate for increased teacher pay and rewards for effective teachers. Follow school board meetings. Advocate for dismissal of teachers who engage in unethical practices and misconduct. Advocate for consistent, relevant professional development to help teachers learn more and teach more effectively. Make your children behave!

Be involved in the initiatives that promote social justice, access to food and nutrition, equal opportunity, access to adult education and fair pay. Advocate for children in public schools to get more services and support available to private schools. Pay attention to local and national education agendas. Be an informed citizen. Vote.

There are countless ways to support education and help eradicate the systemic issues that prevent schools from better serving all children. The ongoing miseducation, especially in high poverty communities, is a social justice issue. To address it, we must address the issues that create it. This exceeds the responsibilities of local school staff. Hunger, abuse, lack of moral support and discipline, poor hygiene, feeling unloved, and other problems students carry in their invisible backpacks require the village, the whole community, to become advocates for radical change. Together, we must completely deconstruct and reassemble how we "do school."

HUDDLE UP!

- Establish school and community partnerships to help parents support student learning and social emotional learning at home.
- Be intentional about finding or creating trauma-based educational sessions to help staff and the community identify signs of abuse, anxiety, and depression.
- Promote and maintain high expectations for both instructional and non-instructional staff engagement in students' school life and learning outcomes, including ownership of problems.
- Don't hesitate to call an emergency time-out for staff to stop doing business as usual, sit down together and grapple with an issue. Allow and encourage staff to propose solutions.

CHAPTER SIX
ADVERSE CLIMATE CONDITIONS

ADVERSE CLIMATE CONDITIONS

In her article addressing the impact of frigid weather on NFL games, sportswriter Allison Koehler explains that cold weather affects the football itself, reducing the air pressure by 20%. She states that a player's grip strength can be cut in half in as little as 15 minutes of being exposed to freezing temperatures. Obviously, this leads to an increase in drops and turnovers. Games played in temperatures 50 degrees and lower see a five percent drop in combined yardage than warm-weather games… and the colder it gets, the greater the impact. Above all, she asserts that in cold weather conditions, the football will not respond as well.[1] Access to advanced technology has a positive impact on school climate conditions. But excessive use of social media adversely affects school life and impedes instruction in the classroom.

Even though I am the youngest of eight children, I was raised like an only child. There is a ten-year age gap between my sister and me. She had graduated and moved ahead with life when I was still quite young. By third grade, I had already grown accustomed to spending countless hours home alone with my imagination, my diary, my schoolbooks and my homework. Mama struggled to keep the bills paid. So, we had the basic necessities, but she could not afford to get the broken television repaired.

I never thought then that I'd someday make this statement: *I am grateful for some of the things I was forced to live without, such as the most popular trendy clothes, freedom to roam the neighborhood, and access to cable television and social media. God used the limitations of my life then to expand it now. The extensive time I spent with my books, the friends I made in the stories I read, and the quality time talking to people in person and on the phone are priceless to me now.*

As an avid reader, I learned about a lot of things I would not have read had I spent hours after school playing video games, watching cable television, and scrolling through social media. Some of my fondest childhood memories were created while spending summers with my older sister and her husband, who had a farm. My nephew and nieces, who were close to my age, were more like cousins, and we played games all day in the "country."

When we got up in the morning, my sister fed us a hot breakfast, then made us do light chores. We had to wash the dishes, sweep the floor, and get clothes off the line. After our chores, all we wanted to do was go outside and stay outside all day long. My sister did not allow too much television, especially in the daytime. She told us soap operas were for grownups. We preferred being outside anyway.

We did not have electronic amenities—cell phones, iPods, iPads, video games and social media. For us, everything exciting and new, interesting and fun, was outside. Outside, we picked berries, bothered the dogs, ran through the cow pasture, and stood by the pigpen reciting *Charlotte's Web*. We dissected frogs on the wooden picnic table. We ate homemade ice cream my sister made outside on the back patio. We picked tomatoes and string beans. We ate watermelon and had contests to see who could spit seeds the farthest. We caught grasshoppers and crickets in a jar during the daytime and caught lightning bugs at night. For sure, those were the good old days.

Many of today's youth, especially in the suburbs and inner cities, have had no such experiences and no such interests. Many of them would rather do anything but go outside. After all, it's hot and there are bugs. They may get dirty. Instead, they prefer to be inside, following social media and playing video games. They don't know their online social life is not authentic. The climate in which students are being reared today has drastically changed over time.

Fingertip access and exposure to *everything out there* all at once is certainly not good for young learners. It has created a completely new and different learning climate for them. It has changed the way they gain and apply new information. They are consistently being distracted and enticed by people and things in the online space.

There seems to be much less emphasis on meeting with friends at a locker, in the gym, and during lunch, and much more emphasis on reviewing their recent social media posts. Online interaction has shifted school climate and culture. Excessive use of social media interferes with instructional time, and it changes the way students think and feel about school life.

SCHOOL CLIMATE

... is the quality and character of school life... the heart and soul of a school...that essence of a school that leads a child, a teacher, and an

administrator to love the school and look forward to being there... It helps them feel socially, emotionally, and physically safe...
—*H. Jerome Freiberg*
School Climate: Measuring, Improving, and Sustaining Healthy Learning Environments[1]

Educators face adverse climate conditions in schools every day. This climate makes it difficult for teachers to do their best work. These conditions limit their ability to catch a pass and run the ball to the end zone. A place where strong relationships are built, exciting learning occurs, and life-long memories are made, in a split second, may become a place where someone is bullied in person and online, or sexually harassed, in person and online. Unfortunately, it is also a place where one may be fatally wounded.

Educators must also contend with the fact that students are not only exposed to the world, but they bring it to school. No matter where students are and what they are doing, as long as they have a phone, there is a separate community, another audience, and an intriguing distraction with them all the time. Far too often, teachers are forced to compete with this new open world climate available to students on social media. Even when they are in class, without a smart device, they may be thinking about what they are missing online.

In a 2018 survey conducted by Pew Research center, 95 percent of teens age 13-17 have a smartphone and almost half of them say they use social media constantly. Over 30 percent say social media has a positive effect on them, mainly because it connects them with friends and family. But 24 percent say it has a negative effect, mostly due to bullying and spreading rumors.[2] In an article addressing the various social issues and struggles of teens, psychotherapist Amy

Morin explains that "teens are facing issues that no previous generation has ever seen. Their social media habits and media consumption are changing the way young people communicate, learn, sleep and exercise."[3]

I remember, back in 2005, the exciting, new online network was Myspace. We've advanced now to Facebook, YouTube, Instagram, Twitter, Snapchat, TikTok and more. But the intent is the same. Everybody gets to have their own space in the cyber world—one in which you can go outside without leaving your home, your bedroom or even your bed. The internet brings parts of the world to you through your fingertips. Online networking also expands teaching and learning beyond the four walls of the classroom, creating opportunities for youth to learn from and with others beyond geographical divides. It connects them, in real-time, with learning centers far across the globe.

Therefore, schools must become "stemified" where science, technology, engineering, and math (STEM) are a central focus of curricula, not just an elective. The value of STEM-based instruction, particularly for girls of color, was so well expressed in the movie *Hidden Figures*. Nominated for three Academy Awards, the film centered on four young Black mathematicians who worked for NASA in the 1950s.[4] Schools are also implementing STEAM curriculum: Science, Technology, Engineering, Arts, and Mathematics.

What I appreciate about technological progress is the opportunity for today's students to learn and see so much more, meet so many more people and experience so many things I did not have at home in rural North Carolina or on the farm in southern Virginia. What concerns me is that the lack of a more controlled learning environment exposes young people to anything and everything inappropriate—not just by choice or curiosity—but also by happenstance. With just one slip of the finger, with one small swipe, they've exposed themselves to information we wish we could unteach them.

Research in 2015 by Turbofuture suggested the average adult spent approximately two hours per day on social media, while teens spent approximately four hours a day. That report also stated that more than 60 percent share their real personal information, such as where they live and go to school and are unaware that this makes them vulnerable to online predators.

Almost 90 percent of the supposedly private, personal sexual photos were stolen and used on pornography sites, without that young person's knowledge and approval. The statistics were connected to the increase in teen suicide, depression, self-hate and various other negative behaviors.[5] More than anything—even when you delete a post—it never goes away. This is one of the most important lessons to teach our children about the cyber world.

In 2018, researchers at the University of Pennsylvania found that limited use of social media lessens loneliness. They found that excessive use leads to depression, which could lead to suicide. While depression, diagnosed or undiagnosed, is a psychological disorder, many young people "feel" oppressed, despondent, ostracized, hopeless and unworthy of being loved.[6] One of the key contributors to young people "feeling depressed" is what they are exposed to on social media. Infatuation with everything happening online has led to a "FOMO" effect, Fear of Missing Out. Young people can't put their phones down for even a few uninterrupted minutes. They are far too afraid of missing out on something.

This new adverse climate persuades them to be "on" and available almost all the time, even in the classroom. Some schools have rules against cell phone use during class, while some teachers have figured out how to incorporate various apps into their lessons to leverage cell phone use for learning. The approach for teachers must not be "if you can't beat them, join them." Instead, it must be "if they want to be online, let's use it as a learning opportunity." Teachers' lack of knowledge and creativity for engaging students online was a huge problem during the pandemic.

Smartsocial.com reports teenagers average more than seven hours on screen in 2019.[7] The time youth spend online is ever increasing. Too much time spent online has adverse effects on their self-esteem and emotional stability. They allow what and who they see on social media to dictate their appearance, influence their relationships, determine their likeability and set the standard for their behavior. Many are more obsessed with online friends and followers —most of whom they do not know and may never meet in person— than they are with real peers they talk to regularly.

While there are certainly benefits to being able to connect across geographical lines and see the wonders of the world through a cell phone, tablet or laptop, there is certainly a downside of being connected abroad without also developing and connecting with one's own local community. We must develop rich, meaningful relationships with people we can see, hear and touch in person. How did young people—or any of us, for that matter—communicate before Facebook, Instagram, Snapchat, YouTube and Twitter? Additional platforms such as TikTok, Clubhouse, and Green Room allows us to make new acquaintances across the globe without ever sitting down to talk face-to-face unless we want to. There are certainly pros and cons to this.

This obsession with being in the online space may be a leading cause of why young people have a negative self-image and engage in cyberbullying—either as the victim or the antagonist. Childhood bullying is a leading risk factor for school-aged children, as its impact can last throughout adulthood. Cyberbullying has become a widespread phenomenon since it increases access and opportunity to bully or be bullied, even in the privacy of a young person's own home.

While bullying was a growing issue among youth before the digital age, it is now much greater and, in some cases, more detrimental. Not only do young people use social media platforms, but they also use direct messaging apps and text messaging to bully each other. They can send threatening messages and accusations, make inflammatory statements, and post embarrassing comments about something another person says or does, as well as how they look or dress.

Michele Hamm, a researcher from the University of Alberta, conducted a review of 36 studies that showed the effects of social media on bullying. Approximately 23 percent of teens reported being targeted for bullying, and 15 percent said they'd bullied someone on social media. Teenagers can misuse social media platforms to spread rumors, share videos aimed at destroying reputations and blackmail others. Hamm's analysis connects bullying to depression, and anxiety, and suggests it can be worse than child abuse.[8]

A good thing about social media is that, in some ways, it may prevent young people from feeling alone. Some of them have difficulty making friends and finding acceptance. Social media gives them global access and an instant sense of community. Sometimes the new community boosts their self-confidence and makes them feel valued.

While the increased access to social media does expose young people to friends across the world they may never meet otherwise, it also exposes them to all sorts of things other young people are doing and offers a wide array of images and behaviors they may choose to emulate. It can easily lead young people to envy a lifestyle they wish they had, even if what they see portrayed online is fabricated. Teens may become obsessed with being like *the person out there* who seems happier, more popular, or more attractive.

Social media connects them to so many people, places, and things which they are often unable to judge what is appropriate or not. They cannot anticipate the grave consequences. They may get pressured by predators who influence them to "show and tell" inappropriate pictures and deeply personal information. Teens and their parents can never be completely sure who "that friend" and follower is.

We've all heard horror stories about boys who tricked girls to make them think they like them or want to take them to the prom—only to learn it was a horrible prank. Or what about the stories where pedophiles coerced young people into posting nude photos, convinced them that they loved them and even arranged to meet and take advantage of them? Often both children and their parents have no idea if these online friends are far away or next door. They don't know if the person is a positive or negative influence and if s/he has a personally dangerous agenda.

In addition to concern about inappropriate connections to strangers, is the concern about exposure teens get from onscreen violence. Gaming, streaming movies and watching television affords them the opportunity to view extremely violent behavior. When we think of the extensive, premeditated violence we see in schools, we must ask ourselves where young people learned these violent behaviors.

Undoubtedly, there are many positive aspects afforded by online connections. Social media access provides opportunities to engage in group thinking, access educational support, gain new knowledge, seek expert advice and strengthen relationships with friends and family across the miles. But the lack of privacy and unawareness of how invasive social media can be when young people's personal lives are on the "big screen" is dangerous. We must teach young people to use discretion and make careful, conscious choices about what to share, when and with whom. Once it's out there, it's out there!

In and of itself, social media has incredibly positive rewards. Technology, and the access it provides, is not the problem. The problem, for youth, is the excessive use of it and the negative impact it has on them, their school life, and their families. Parents must closely monitor the other life their children may have online. They must make time for family gatherings and face-to-face interaction with their children. Children need to experience no social media zones and a device shut off time every day. More emphasis must be placed on literacy, in-person social engagement, and mindfulness.

Teachers must become more astute in how to use social media and other technology resources to enhance instruction. They must become leaders in the virtual learning world and embrace classroom connections across the globe. They must explore new, strategic ways to use technology for student engagement and assessment. All of this must be included both in teacher preparation coursework and school-based professional development for teachers.

HUDDLE UP!

- Provide teachers with professional development on how to use technology and social media for instruction and positive student engagement.
- Provide students with information on appropriate use of technology as well as cyber bullying and abuse. Ensure that students are aware of the dangers.
- Hold staff to high expectations for ethics and encourage them to be careful and intentional about what/how they share their personal lives online.

CHAPTER SEVEN
NO ONE CALLED A FOUL ON THE PLAY

PENALTY FLAG

This is a yellow scarf the referee throws down on the field when a player breaks a rule of the game such as holding a player back, interfering with a pass, playing unnecessarily rough, and false starts. There are different flags but the yellow one means there is a penalty with consequences for foul play. Students must fully understand what their rights are and what the consequences are for foul play in their lives. When someone holds them the wrong way, interferes with their space and safety, handles them roughly, or just crosses the line, violators should be exposed and reported.

"Don't let boys mess with you," Mama said, "...because if you get pregnant, I'm putting you out of this house." That was my simple introduction to "the birds and the bees." But I knew not to go there. Perhaps it was a blessing that we did not have a working television at home, so I could not learn what adults do in the bedroom from television.

When I was five years old, my father came home occasionally to "visit" my mother. They were in the bedroom so long that I went to the door to knock. I asked if I could enter. But my mother didn't hear me or realize she had left the bedroom door ajar, so I peeked in. I couldn't figure out what they were doing, but it looked strange. I was afraid to ask her about it later for fear I would be chastised for looking. Something about what I saw made me feel, like my parents were doing something bad. People do bad things behind closed doors. I also felt very confused. I wanted to ask my mother later, "What in the world were you doing?"

When I was seven years old, a family friend introduced me to a game called "Sneaky Peeky." Children love hide-and-seek and other games that involve sneaking around. So, I was eager to learn the game. I hid in the dark. Once he found me, he made me get undressed in front of him and just stand there. He didn't touch me; he just closely examined every single part of me—my skin, birthmark, breasts, legs, etc. After prolonged periods of staring, he gave me criticism and compliments.

He told me I could never tell anyone because it was a sneaky game. Telling anyone else would take the fun part out of it. He also said I would get in really big trouble and probably get a whipping. That created double trauma because I was extremely uncomfortable playing the game against my will, and I was terrified of getting a whipping. For some reason, I forgot the compliments, but I remembered the criticism. Sneaky Peeky made me feel embarrassed, dirty and ugly. I never told my mother about this.

According to the National Center for Victims of Crime, "A child who is the victim of prolonged sexual abuse usually develops low self-esteem, a feeling of worthlessness and an abnormal or distorted view of sex. The child may become withdrawn and mistrustful of adults and can become suicidal.... Child sexual abuse is not solely restricted to physical contact; such abuse could include noncontact abuse, such as exposure, voyeurism and child pornography."[1]

When I was nine, I was at the home of another family friend, playing with a ball. When it rolled under the bed, I crawled under to get it. I saw several magazines with naked men on the cover. Inside were lots of naked men with erections. At that age, I didn't know what an erection is. I wanted to ask about the pictures, but I was afraid I would be accused of searching under the bed without permission. The pictures made me feel sick. I couldn't figure out how every man walked around like *that*.

All three of these experiences prematurely exposed me to sexuality. They were detrimental not only because of violation and neglect but also because I was afraid to talk to anyone about it.

It is natural for children to inquire about things that are interesting or strange to them. It's important for parents to create a safe space for children to ask for information without fear of being chastised or judged.

When I was twelve years old, some friends at school were debating if a girl can get pregnant if she has sex during her menstrual cycle. We could not agree on an answer. We didn't dare ask the teacher, and I knew better than to ask my mother. So, I wrote a letter to my sister who was in active duty in Germany at the time. It felt like forever waiting to get a response by mail to come all the way from Germany on a question I could not utter at home. But she wrote me back, and I was able to share my informed opinion at school.

When a child asks about why adults do *that*, Meg Hickling,

retired nurse and award-winning educator advises parents to explain, "Some grown-ups enjoy that kind of activity. When you're a grown-up, you get to decide what you want to do." She recommends that parents tell their children to share information they see, hear, or find online and ask questions about what they don't understand.[2]

Children's lives are filled with foul play that nobody calls. Either no referee was there, or the referee wasn't paying close attention. We must throw the penalty flag every time a foul is made; then stop the game to address it. We must teach children what their rights are and what to do if they feel their rights are violated.

After the don't-mess-with-boys conversation with my mother, I wanted clarity. But I knew not to ask for it. Was messing with boys the same as "wrestling" in bed like she did with my dad? Was it taking off my clothes for Sneaky Peeky? Was it what men were pictured doing in the magazine? I really didn't know what she meant by "messing with boys." But I decided not to get any closer to boys than absolutely necessary, to avoid the mess. I was never sure what the rules were regarding "messing with girls," either. But I figured that one out on my own.

So that I wouldn't be alone all day, my mother allowed a neighborhood friend to come over to play with me while she worked on Saturdays. I liked playing "classroom," but she liked playing "doctor's office." My idea of playing doctor was looking in her eyes, ears and nose, hitting her knee with a ruler, listening to her heartbeat and writing her a prescription—all things that didn't require undressing. But her idea included that and more. She suggested we "take off our pants and feel around" for diseases. When I didn't agree with that idea, she suggested we get in bed naked and lay close to each other. I immediately made her leave the house. I told my mom she couldn't come over anymore because she bossed me around and ate all the cereal. Mama could not afford to buy *extra* cereal.

Later that year, I learned my neighbor friend was pregnant.

While I had a good guess as to *how* that happened, I wasn't able to wrap my head around *why* she would let it happen. It made no sense to me why any friend my age would want a real baby that cries all the time and has to be changed and fed. But Mama said my friend was "too grown" and for me to stay away from her. My friend did not come back to school in the Fall. But much later in life, I learned she had suffered repeated sexual abuse by her mother's boyfriend. I assume he taught her how to play "doctor's office" and "feel around for diseases."

I was well into my teenage years when I developed an even more warped understanding of sexuality. I learned bits and pieces about sex from friends at school and from context clues while watching soap operas. But, at least, I understood *something*. I eventually read about it in *Harlequin Romance* novels, which a classmate stole from her mom's room and brought to me at school once she finished reading them. I could not put them down, but I certainly kept them hidden from my mother.

Times have certainly changed. During my youth, most children were limited in their learning about sex because the internet wasn't available. Television shows actually followed guidelines about nudity and lewdness. The sex education class at school consisted of a three-day curriculum, one hour per day, during which the school nurse explained menstruation, conception, and birth, as well as how a condom prevents teenage pregnancy at 99% and abstinence at 100%. She also explained syphilis, gonorrhea and herpes. That's it.

Whose job is it to teach children about sex? When? Where? How much do they need to know? Parents, school leaders and even churches need to deal with sexuality so that children don't first learn about it from peers at school, social media, and unhealthy experimentation. We need to teach them about their own bodies, using the correct terminology for body parts. We need not make it awkward, funny or taboo to say the proper name of the sexual anatomy. They need to understand the value and benefits of celibacy and abstinence, as well as the physical and spiritual connection that sex creates.

This is what I tell teenagers. "We were created with sexual bodies and sexual organs. Our bodies were created to elicit a sexual response to sexual stimuli. One does not have to act on that response, nor does one have to share, deny or reject it. It is a normal response! The response your body emits during a sexual act, whether you engaged in sex voluntarily or through abuse, is a normal, natural phenomenon. Awakening and eliciting this response too soon, involuntarily, and with the wrong person may have confusing and long-term effects on who you are and who you are becoming."

I tell them, "Be very careful with experimentation and curiosity so you don't develop an overwhelming and, in some cases, inordinate or insatiable appetite." It is both my professional and personal recommendation that we encourage them to abstain from sex until adulthood, a time when the can make mature decisions. But sometimes telling a young person what to do is not as effective as teaching them how to think. Ultimately, we want them to learn how to make good decisions. We want them to think through the problems, options, rewards, and consequences of their actions.

When I was teaching ninth graders, I had a student who longed to be liked and accepted. I *heard* that she had a reputation of providing a "special service" (in the boys' bathroom) for a small fee. I wrote her a note that said, "Every time you do them a sexual favor, you're receiving an emotional deposit you can't just wipe off. I'd hate to see you carry a small part of all of them with you for the rest of your life. Let me know if you want to talk about this."

I slipped the note to her in class while passing out graded papers. She seemed shocked and embarrassed for the rest of class. But I gave her space to sit with her thoughts, consider consequences, and determine next step possibilities. When class was over, I told her I cared about her and believed she could make much better choices for her life. I told her she was worth so much more than *that*. I offered to listen and talk about anything she wanted to ask or share.

I did not know the boys involved in these activities, but I knew the girl. The moment I was made aware of the offensive foul, I became accountable. Some educators would look away because they think this is not their business and because they cannot not save the world. This is true. They feel they get paid to teach and nothing else. This is not true. We get paid to teach the students, not content. We must know the students and understand how they think so we can teach them well. So, I acted; I refused to be complicit. *I called a foul on the play.*

Based on what I knew about this girl's family, calling her parents could have made the matter much worse. Giving her a private note was a much more powerful approach than yelling and condemning her. I didn't want to reprimand her or make her feel ashamed. I wanted to make her think. That was a conscious intentional approach because I understood the team's goal: *just get the football into the end zone.*

Writing a disciplinary referral for suspension seldom ensures behavior adjustment. Given that I learned about the incident eavesdropping on the hallway gossip between classes, I had limited information. I did notify the principal of the rumors, without telling him I thought they were true. He assigned bathroom monitors during and between classes. The good news is that I never heard about any other "events" in the bathroom. I was there when she graduated high school with dignity, self-respect and a better reputation. She wrote a note and thanked me for "the talk."

We must deal with issues of sexuality and talk to young people about their interests and intentions. They are growing up in a very liberal, media-driven, openly sexual society. Instead, we need to be open and honest with them about good and bad choices, consequences and rewards, and what they may intentionally, or even unintentionally, invite into their lives that could, in some ways, damage their destiny.

They have interests, urges, curiosities and legitimate feelings—the same as we had when we were their age. We have to stop reprimanding them and talk to them sooner rather than later about what's going on in their minds and hearts. What causes them to be confused about their sexual identity? What causes them to degrade themselves? What causes them to demand negative attention or look for love in all the wrong places? What's happening on the inside eventually shows itself on the outside. But if we can do the hard part —which is helping them get the inside decluttered and cleaned up— then dealing with the outside becomes the easy part. We must address their thinking, not only their behavior.

When we talk to young people about sex, the talks should not just be about what not to do and what diseases they could get. They need to understand puberty, hormones, love, and emotions. They need to know sexual feelings are normal but should be reserved for the right time. They need to understand who should be allowed to touch them sexually, when and why.

As old-fashioned as it may seem, they need to understand the sanctity of marriage and the beauty of sharing that *first time* with someone they deeply love, so it doesn't become a common thing to do with anyone, anytime, without consequences, as portrayed online and on television. They also need to understand birth control, including but not limited to abstinence. They need nonjudgement and freedom to ask any question and get advice on how to make good decisions, especially when under pressure. More importantly, they need to understand their right to say "no."

In school, students should be taught that their bodies belong to them and no one should pressure them into doing anything they don't want to do. According to the Centers for Disease Control's *National Youth Risk Behavior Survey,* only 20 percent of middle schools and 40 percent of high schools provide instruction regarding sexual health. Students need to learn how to avoid unhealthy, high-risk behaviors.[3] They need information, presented by a trained health instructor who can present it in ways that engage them in critical thinking, self-reflection, and responsible decision-making.

The Center reports that among high school students in 2019, approximately 40 percent reported they'd had sexual intercourse. Ten percent reported having had four or more partners and seven percent had been forced to have sex against their will. Almost 30 percent had sexual intercourse within three months prior to completing the survey and almost 50 percent of them did not use a condom. More than ten percent did not use any other form of birth control. Sadly, over 20 percent had experienced sexual intercourse in conjunction with drugs and alcohol.[4]

It is important for students to understand how to avoid sexually transmitted diseases and unplanned pregnancies. They need to understand sexual rights, recognize when lines have been crossed, and know when and how to report abuse. Premature exposure to sex coupled with lack of proper sexual health education may lead to illicit sexual behavior, multiple partners, unprotected sexual activity, lower academic performance, confusion, and depression. It is not surprising that grappling with these issues alone, and perhaps in shame, may also lead to drug and alcohol use or even suicide.

Schools bear some of the responsibility in recognizing and appropriately responding to known *fouls on the play* regarding student misconduct and abuse of any kind. But schools need adequate staffing and community support to address issues raised in this chapter. School leaders need *access* to guidance counselors, social workers, psychologists, nurses, and other support staff so they, together, can create an extension of instructional services that will greatly impact the educational and personal development of students with varied levels of understanding.

HUDDLE UP!

- Encourage staff to create space, in assignments, group events, and one-on-one conversations, for students to share their feelings and ask for information without fear of being chastised or judged.
- Supportive adults must talk to young people about sexual development, assault, and health so they understand when lines are crossed and know what to do when and if violated.
- Lobby for educators to get the necessary training to identify and appropriately respond to any student trauma made known to them. Display help center hotline information in your school.
- To the extent that you are allowed, based on your district or state policies, provide students of age with sexual health information from a trained health instructor.
- Make sure other support providers such as school nurse, psychologist, resource officer, counselor, testing coordinators, and social workers understand your school values and fully support your school's end zone strategy for social emotional learning, wellness, and safety.

CHAPTER EIGHT
PASS INTERFERENCE

PASS INTERFERENCE

...is a foul that occurs when a defensive player interferes with a receiving player's opportunity or attempt to catch an incoming pass. Teachers are prepared to receive a student in class and then provide both the instruction and interventions to get that student into the end zone. But sometimes their efforts are thwarted. Various school practices, procedures, and policies interfere with teachers' ability to catch a complete pass. Zero tolerance policies and other punitive practices cause interferences that thwart students' opportunities to succeed.

When I was a high school teacher, there was a student who exemplified everything a teacher would define a model student to be. He had excellent grades. He was a star athlete and held an office in student government. He was kind, honest, hardworking, and liked by peers and faculty.

One morning as he was preparing to drive to school, his car would not start. His parents had already left for work. There was no other car at the home (during this pre-Uber era). Determined to be on time, he ran across the field to his grandfather's house. His grandfather agreed to get the car running for him and drop it off at the school later. "But in the meantime," his grandfather said, "take my truck so you won't be late." The student jumped into his grandfather's pick-up truck, drove to school, and got to class just seconds before the bell rang.

A couple hours later, he was called to the office and questioned about the rifle in the truck. In his rush to get to school on time, the student never paid attention to the gun his grandfather had left in his truck after he had been hunting the day before. The student had absolutely no intention of using the gun, no intention to harm anyone at school and no idea the gun was in the truck. The school resource officer asked him whether it was loaded. He was expelled from the school and the school district for the rest of the school year for bringing a weapon on school premises.

In the early 1990s, several state leaders in education began to enforce severe consequences for students (or anyone) in possession of a firearm on school grounds. Policies were developed across school districts to ensure persons whose behavior threatened the safety and well-being of others were permanently expelled from not only the local school but the entire school district, and sometimes all schools in the state.

In addition to possession of firearms, the policies in many locales also included possession of knives and anything else that could be deemed a weapon. The fact that the policy demanded absolutely no mercy or second chances for various student behaviors is why even well-intended or uninformed students in a precarious situation, such as the aforementioned young man, received the greatest punishment, regardless of motive or rationale or extenuating circumstances.

The zero-tolerance policy of the school district had to be enforced, resulting in this student being expelled. His parents were able to get him enrolled in a different district in the state, where he was able to finish his senior year. The school principal fought long and hard (and was successful) at getting the local and state school boards to approve allowing the student to return to school grounds on graduation day. He was able to participate in commencement exercises with his graduating class.

While the violation of the possession of firearms policy was clearly evident, the zero-tolerance approach dismissed any consideration of the student's extenuating circumstances and fostered no opportunity for restoration—even though there was no negative intent, no harm done to anyone, and no record of any previous misconduct.

He received the most severe punishment—not because of what happened—but because of what could have happened. While I understand the zero-tolerance policy was designed to protect students and teachers overall, it had proven to be severely, unjustly punitive for students whose behavior does not necessarily warrant such harsh consequences.

Policies enforcing zero-tolerance ensure the strictest punishment of students who break a rule and commit a crime. The idea is that the assurance of these severe consequences will deter any student from crossing the line, even unintentionally. The American Bar Association[1] opposed these policy mandates for school suspension and expulsion because they were being enforced without consideration for situational context and rationale. In 2001, they passed a resolution stating that zero-tolerance policies lead to discrimination and/or dictate harsh punishment, without regard for the circumstantial nature of the "crime" and the student's prior history.

This is exactly why the model student mentioned in this chapter deserved a second chance. While bringing a gun to school for any reason is clearly wrong, the specific circumstances, and the student's positive record of behavior, should have been considered. While it's wrong, was it intentional? He was not even aware that his grandfather's hunting rifle was in the rack of the truck. He was completely unaware a rifle was in his possession.

While it is wrong to bring drugs to school, is it a crime for a preteen to give a friend headache medication, if requested? If both girls agreed, and both sets of parents agreed there was no harm done, does the zero-tolerance policy really apply? Have the girls committed a crime?

What about the cases of bullying wherein both the pursuant and the victim who fights back get expelled on the basis of no tolerance? So, if a student hits a victim, and that victimized student hits back, both have violated the policy and both get expelled. Is the victim's appropriate option then to *not* defend himself to avoid being expelled?

Zero-tolerance policies allow no forgiveness or forbearance for self-defense—even when a well-behaved student with good grades has been bullied and provoked to protect himself. Many people have been critical of zero-tolerance policies, claiming that they are overly draconian, provide little if any benefit to anyone, contribute to overcrowding of the criminal justice system and/or disproportionately target Blacks and Latinos.

In his blog post, author Nick Gillespie provides an account of a Texan ninth-grader who was arrested for bringing a homemade clock to school, which teachers thought to be a mock bomb; a second-grader from Maryland who pointed a Pop-Tart at a classmate after nibbling it into the shape of a toy gun; and an eighth-grader from Washington who was expelled for "drug use" because she gave a Midol tablet to a friend who had menstrual cramps.[2]

Gillespie asserts that: "Zero-tolerance policies in public K-12 schools... have no real benefit and significant adverse effects... Boys are punished about twice as often as girls and Blacks and Hispanics about 50 percent more often than Whites...Over 75 percent of school districts have a zero-tolerance policy... without ever assessing whether the policies actually reduce violence and aid education.[3]

Zero-tolerance policies are also enforced as a means of ridding schools of drugs. But some states have seen an actual increase in drug use since instituting harsh consequences. While most states in the U.S. have adopted these policies that lead to extended suspension and expulsion, few have alternative education policies in place to ensure these students have an opportunity to continue learning. This perpetuates a vicious cycle because, having been expelled, students have trouble getting reacclimated, upon return to the school environment and classroom curriculum.

They are not given ample opportunity nor the individualized instruction necessary to catch up on what they missed so they can move forward with the next unit of study. Many are also picked on by peers and humiliated by teachers who are aware of their suspensions. This puts them in self-defense mode and leads to further behavioral issues.

Students expelled within the first trimester of the school year have little to no chance of getting back on track academically. So, they spend the remaining six months of a traditional school year barely staying afloat or they just fall too far behind to even care. This certainly does not teach the lesson for which zero-tolerance policies were designed. They do not teach violators to change their behavior. Instead, they inadvertently encourage more of it.

This is a clear example of pass interference—preventing teachers and other school staff from *keeping the ball in play*. How can they get students in the end zone if policies are instituted that keep students from having a chance to succeed? Often there is no recovery for students whose lives are interrupted by disciplinary actions determined without considerations of their various circumstances, and without respect for the situational context of an offense. Albeit teachers may be poised to support and defend the student charged, they can't receive and run the ball if there is ongoing pass interference.

Since the 1990s, educators seem to have bought into the idea that these policies were designed to protect the good students from the bad ones. That is a flawed philosophy. Behavior is learned best through modeling—good or bad. There is also no compelling evidence that moving perceived trouble-making students out of the educational system into the juvenile system increases learning and makes school safer.

When students are permanently removed from school, they are then unable to learn from interactions with peers. They receive little to no coaching on how to think about their actions and examine consequences. Infusing social emotional learning and mindfulness strategies into curriculum is critical for their success. When self-correction is not taught or modeled at home, school faculty can address it *on the field*.

Instructional leaders know what it takes to get students to the end zone. But they can't do this when policies prevent us from making *interceptions*. One way for teachers to *intercept* students is to gather as an inquiry team and examine all forms of student data, both behavioral and academic. Once they determine the "learning interference problem" and its root cause, they assess what works well or not for this student(s) and create a plan to address the problem(s) and get the student back on track. The inquiry cycle[4] (or school-based problem solving) helps prevent fumbles.

Part of a good education is understanding good behavior and good citizenship. When schools include restorative justice in the curriculum, teachers and students learn restorative practices. These social emotional strategies help students to self-correct behaviors, process conflicts amicably and focus on empathy and accountability. I have found that enforcing zero-tolerance rather than educating students on self-management does not increase school safety; it often leads to legal punishment for harmless and/or unintentional offenses and increases the likelihood of suspended youth being home alone (due to working parents).

SUSPENSION AND EXPULSION

Suspension is the temporary removal of a student from both the classroom and all other school activities. When expelled, a student is permanently removed from school and/or the district due to serious, dangerous offenses.

Suspension and expulsion from school is a punishment that perpetuates miseducation. It has adverse effects on other areas of a young person's life. It creates a cycle whereby students misbehave, get kicked out, and receive zeroes for most, if not all, of their assignments they missed while suspended. They aren't remediated upon return to school, then they misbehave again because they feel left behind in the classroom and can't get the work done (even if they wanted to). As frustration builds, they misbehave again, and the cycle keeps repeating itself.

Many teachers give preferential treatment to White students, without realizing it. Suspending disorderly students from school is often the first response of White teachers. Across the U.S., students of color continue to be more often suspended and expelled, which means they are punished more harshly for their misbehaviors than White students. This is how the school pipeline to prison system began.

Jacqueline Jordan Irvine suggested, "One factor related to the nonachievement of Black students is the disproportionate use of severe disciplinary practices, which leads to Black students' exclusion from classes, their perceptions of mistreatment and feelings of alienation and rejection, which result ultimately in their misbehaving more and/or leaving school."[5]

Both zero-tolerance policies and the school-to-prison pipeline are institutional practices that disproportionately affect equitable schooling for students of color. The school-to-prison pipeline includes excessively harsh practices such as zero-tolerance policies, increased referrals for disciplinary actions, misdiagnosed special education codes, high stakes testing and the frequency of suspension and expulsion. All of these create a pathway down which students of color, especially boys, are pushed. These practices interfere with the efforts of supportive teachers and school leaders who fight for equity and restorative justice in consideration of students' lived experiences and growth potential.

Academic pass interference may occur as a result of bad policy. It occurs in schools when both teachers and athletic coaches are denied the autonomy, opportunity or flexibility to do what is in the best interest of "this student at this time." "These students at this time" is a concept I learned as I was pursuing National Board Certification,[6] a performance-based independent assessment of teaching practice.

Part of the assessment process in completing my portfolio

required that I provide clear, concise and consistent evidence of instructional decision-making that was appropriate for the specific students in my class, given all of their varied learning needs and backgrounds. The freedom National Board Certification fostered in allowing and challenging me to teach and do what my students needed, the way they needed it (based on pedagogical knowledge and justifiable proof that it was in the best interests of *this specific learner at this particular time*) was so liberating for me as a young teacher.

It helped me understand the difference between equality and equity. Equality is mostly put forth as sameness, meaning all students get the same, exact teaching and disciplinary handling. But equitable teaching demanded that I be more intentional about how I serve students individually and become more aware of how they synthesize information. This includes how it relates to their lived experiences, how it may influence their behavior, and the impact it may have on further learning.

Teaching Greg Lockhart, ninth grader by day and punk rock star by imagination, was the highlight of my early career. He wore black nail polish and lipstick. He had a jet-black mohawk. He wore grunge clothing, had several piercings and tattoos, and refused to carry textbooks. I never made a big deal out of his appearance because effective teachers don't do that. When he asked me what I thought about how he looked, I told him he looked like a poet.

I gave him a few different assignments from what I gave the rest of the class because he was a more advanced thinker. I assigned readings I knew would interest him. He and I had one-on-one literature reviews at the beginning or end of class. His mother told me she was shocked to see him enjoying the readings because he had been so disinterested in other classes.

Greg informed me he was dropping out at the end of the semester when he would be old enough to get his GED (Graduate

Equivalency Degree). I made a strong argument for why he should stay based on all the really cool stuff he would never read about if he didn't stick around for me to share it with him. After much prodding, he finally agreed. "But only your class, Miss O, and that's it." I thought he meant he would only do the work in my class, and not that of his other classes.

By ninth grade, he had made up his mind that school is a place where he does not fit in and where teachers don't care about him. He felt irrelevant, unprovocative assignments were a waste of his intellect and his time. He never actually told me he felt this way. I figured it out. And I'm glad I figured it out early in the semester, after our first few one-on-one chats. I was ready for a student like Greg. I felt like NFL wide receiver Terrell Owens who always said, "If you put the ball in my hands, there's a better chance of winning." I was *not* going to lose Greg; I was *not* going to fumble!

A few weeks later, the principal informed me that Greg was attending only my first-period class and leaving school afterward. I pleaded with him, "You cannot suspend this kid!" I had *intercepted* Greg, and no one was going to keep me from getting him into the end zone. Greg *wanted* to be in my class because I was the only teacher who really saw him, beyond the grunge. What teenager gets up and comes all the way to school, to sit through a 90-minute English class and then leave and walk home, every day? Who does that? Greg did that.

I was getting through to him and he was enjoying learning. The principal relented and Greg was able to stay. The lesson here is that I wasn't just teaching English, I was teaching Greg. And to make up for all the other teachers who could not "see" Greg, I had to provide intellectually rich, culturally relevant lessons for him every day. It worked!

School attendance policy mandated that Greg be expelled for excessive truancy. Put the student out for being out—makes perfect sense, right? But my principal granted me the chance to give Greg a chance, one that was long overdue. The principal made a complete pass to me and I kept running toward the end zone. Zero-tolerance policies, which include suspension and expulsion, are acts of equality, rather than equity. Every student who crosses certain lines, even unintentionally, with or without provocation, gets the exact same harsh treatment. There is no consideration of what may be best for *this student at this time.*

These policies create pass interferences between those who know a student academically and personally and those who don't. When a teacher stands up for a student in support of his or her academic needs and personal rights, that teacher deserves the opportunity to get in position for a complete pass, without interference.

HUDDLE UP!

- Pay attention to the detrimental and/or discriminatory effect of zero-tolerance on circumstantial missteps of students with no prior negative history. Advocate for equity and restorative justice in consideration of students' lived experiences and growth potential.
- Advocate for forgiveness and forbearance of inappropriate behaviors when students have been bullied and/or provoked to protect themselves.
- In the event of short-term suspension, respect that the punishment is complete once student return to school and ensure that adequate social and academic support is provided to get students back on track academically.
- Learn the inquiry cycle and teach it to your school leadership team. Implement a train-the-trainer model so that members of your initial inquiry team may train all departments or grade level teams. Expect all staff, including noninstructional staff, to use the cycle of

inquiry to determine next step actions for students who need academic and/or behavioral intervention.
- Arrange ongoing professional development that includes restorative practices, behavior modification strategies, asset-based instruction for high-need students, and cultural responsiveness to students' learning differences and family backgrounds.
- Provide students with coaching on how to think about their actions and examine consequences. Include social emotional learning and mindfulness strategies in the curriculum.

CHAPTER NINE
COMPLETELY DEFLATED FOOTBALLS

DEFLATED FOOTBALLS

According to Wikipedia, the footballs must be inflated to an air pressure between 12.5 and 13.5 pounds per square inch and must be available for the referee to test with a pressure gauge before the game. Without enough air pressure, the football would be deflated, which makes it difficult to pass, catch, kick, and punt. Damage and excessive pressure on the ball can cause it to become deflated. Parents and educators must talk to students to understand what stressors cause them to feel deflated or depressed.

Teaching would be such an easy job if all students showed up on the first day of school having met the desired regulations and specifications, sealed in a special box, and shipped directly to the classroom from a manufacturer. It would be great if every student had a specific regulated social emotional "pressure" so teachers would always know what to expect and be able to handle each student's needs appropriately.

But teaching continues to be a profession wherein new teachers are held to the same performance expectations on day one as a teacher with five years of experience. They are expected to pass, catch, kick and run the ball, not matter how deflated or damaged it may be. There's no "drive-thru" offer available; teachers don't get to pick who and what they want to teach.

I grew up with a lot of anxiety. Living with barely enough, my mother constantly worried about what would happen next. I, too, worried about bad things happening. I worried my mother's stress would result in a heart attack, or that her suicidal thoughts and attempts would one day be successful. I worried about someone breaking into the house, where I was often home alone. I worried that my absentee father's visits, few and far between, would stop altogether, that we would completely lose contact, and that he would not be there on my wedding day. Even worse, I worried that he would die, and I wouldn't even know about it.

Daily, I prayed that my grades, as perfect as I tried to make them, would be enough to get me a college scholarship. I desperately wanted to be a teacher. I was excited about what college would mean for me—a first generation, four-year college bound, young Black girl from the "boondocks." My mother often threatened to make me go to the military. This always bothered me. When our television was working, I watched *Hogan's Heroes* and *M.A.S.H.* thinking there's no way I'm cut out for this.

School leaders and teachers who engage in meaningful conversations with their students to allow them to talk about what's bothering them are better positioned to serve their needs. Providing students with a safe space to discuss their problems and share their personal truth, is a positive way to boost their confidence and help them cope with various challenges. If perhaps once, just once, a teacher had asked me about my fears and concerns regarding my future, it may have lessened my anxiety. Perhaps s/he could have made suggestions about how to handle my fears or helped me think through all the options life would have for me.

High school principal Renee Hood posted this comment[1] in a Facebook group for educators. (Reprinted with permission) *I had a very interesting and enlightening conversation with a 10th-grade honors student who came to my office. I took the opportunity to ask her a few questions. Here are her answers:*

- What is the increasing appeal of vaping with your age group? *It helps with stress and anxiety, but it is leading kids to drugs more. I've seen a lot of my friends start with vaping and move to pot and other drugs. It's all about finding relief from anxiety. Everybody, just about, has tried it.*
- Why is your generation so stressed out—more anxious than kids even five to seven years ago? *I think social media is the reason everyone is anxiety-ridden. There is no relief and it's worse than any of the adults think it is. Bullying, harassment, nude pix and just mean stuff is all over social media and texting every day. We'd rather see what is on it, so we aren't blindsided, than to close our accounts and not know what's being said about us. It's invading every minute of our lives, but we can't go without it.*

- What can we (school personnel) do to help? *We need therapists at school, not just counselors. Therapy dogs, too. I'm not sure schools can really help. We're too far gone to survive our teens. Parents are just as stressed out and addicted to social media as we are.*

I can't imagine how many teenagers are feeling as though they are "too far gone to survive." Is this what happened at Columbine and Douglas high schools? Were the teenaged shooters too far gone? Is this why Hannah Baker[2] committed suicide after making cassette recordings about thirteen people who contributed to her feeling completed deflated. Was Hannah's situation too far gone?

Like Renee, every school leader (and parents, too) should take time to talk and really listen to students. Listening to students without judging them is critically important because they may be experiencing extreme stress and suffering in silence. Renee, as a principal, demonstrates the character and welcoming spirit she expects teachers in her building to demonstrate. The information gained from the conversation with this student informs the work of the school staff and influences the school's culture for learning.

In her book, *The Deepest Well*, pediatrician Nadine Burke Harris writes about the effect of adverse childhood experiences and toxic stress for children, from birth to age 18. She explains the impact of trauma on a child's physical and psychological development.[3] Her work helps us understand how anxiety, neglect, and abuse cause health issues.

Her medical practice and research have exposed how systemic issues such as domestic abuse and homelessness may cause lung and/or heart problems. Her work garnered the attention and support of former First Lady Hillary Clinton and Vice President Kamala Harris. Adverse childhood experiences at home and at school should not be taken lightly. Trauma-based education must be included in educator preparation coursework and ongoing school-based professional development for all staff.

Understanding Stress in Academic Settings

Stress is more broadly defined as a *condition* of extreme difficulty, pressure or psychological strain in response to adverse events. Stress is capable of causing physical damage. There are three kinds of stress:

1. Positive stress—when something good is going to happen, like getting ready for prom or graduation, which elicits good hormones
2. Tolerable stress—when a situation is not good, but you can handle it, like missing a flight, pressure to finish a project on a deadline, or preparing for an audition
3. Toxic stress—when something bad happens, causing overwhelming fear or frustration and/or difficulty coping, often resulting in sickness such as insomnia, digestive issues and/or respiratory conditions

Toxic stress is chronic stress. It affects the body in many ways. It can cause insomnia, stomach problems, mental confusion, eating disorders, lethargy, and joint pain. It can also lead to clinical depression, heart disease, obesity and substance abuse.

Adults often assume that young people do not have significant stressors because they don't have household bills and debts, aren't facing marital challenges, or just don't have much life responsibility. But there are heavy stressors in the lives of youth and young adults, including peer pressure, bullying, the desire to fit in, low self-esteem, lack of attention at home, sexual identity questions, poverty, and more.

These are some of the issues that cause stress. Yet, these and other issues, such as anger, eating disorders, bullying, promiscuity, teen pregnancy, substance abuse and suicide are also perpetuated by stress. Young people worry about things. Thinking about whether their parents are going to get divorced or if they will have the money for college may cause serious mental anguish. They worry about being popular in school, being able to pass a test, and being ostracized by peers.

Not only does stress negatively affect students, but also teachers. I was affected by the stress my students experienced. Once, a student told me she was pregnant and could not tell her mother. One of my students was shot, as an innocent bystander, after a football game. Another student found his brother after school, having hung himself in the closet.

Another student never finished her homework because every day after school, she cleaned the house and made dinner for her dad and younger siblings then helped them do their homework. She said her mother was drunk every night. I knew her mother, so I was surprised. When I asked for clarification, she said, "Like I said, my mother is an alcoholic. She comes home from work and gets drunk every night because my father is a jerk!"

These real-life circumstances were stressful for my students and for me. For many of them, I had to be more than a teacher. I could not just "leave it all at work." I worried about them and their families. Writer Alexandra Sifferlin states, "Teachers who experience higher levels of burnout report to be more stressed, less effective in teaching and classroom management, less connected to their students and less satisfied with their work."[4]

"There is a lot of emotional stress that people go through. Some

people figure out a way to handle it. They have a strong enough support system to keep going and keep moving forward. And some people, they feel like they don't have that outlet."
—Terrell Owens, NFL Hall of Fame

Even though I became overworked and burned out as I shared in the stress of my students, I always made sure I created a safe, open environment for them to talk to me. I think stressful situations worsen when young people feel they have no one to talk to. I admonish adults to resist what I call "the shock factor." Don't react in shock when young people share their secrets with you. Create an open space for them to share what's really going on with them. Don't be so judgmental. You were once a teen.

Young people often complain to me about how adults develop selective amnesia when it comes to their own mistakes of the past. Part of the work I do is to educate teachers, parents and pastors on *how to listen* to youth. I also advocate for zillennials, the "up to 24" group. Most of them aren't as mature as they think they are. They need role models who are authentically open and forthright about their mistakes in life.

They need to be able to tell you they smoked a cigarette—or something else—or that they don't like something or someone. They need to be able to tell you if they have uncomfortable thoughts or urges. Maybe they want to have sex. Maybe they hate their life. Maybe they aren't sure if they are attracted to boys or girls, or *both*.

What would be your first reaction if a young person shared this with you? Hopefully, you won't respond in a way that causes them to feel ashamed, exposed or unloved. Respond the way you want people to respond to you. The young person talking to you is stressed. You can either perpetuate it or help them cope with it, exacerbate it or help eradicate it. Be quick to listen and slow to lecture.

Another major stressor among young people is test anxiety. The pressure to do well or even just to pass standardized tests is deflating. Whether they are a struggling learner who is frustrated by testing, an apathetic student who refuses to study because they see no relevance in the content, or an overachiever who feels their future hinges on high test scores, all students feel the pressure. Because test results are used to label and categorize students, both they and their teachers feel extraordinary pressure to perform on demand. Inability to do so pushes both teachers and students out of the educational system. Thought leader Alfie Kohn asserts:

"...The intellectual life is being squeezed out of schools... as tests take over the curriculum. Punitive consequences are being meted out on the basis of manifestly inadequate and inappropriate exams. Children are literally becoming sick with fear over their scores. Massive numbers of students—particularly low income and minority students—may be pushed out of school altogether."[5]
—*Alfie Kohn, The Case Against Standardized Testing*

As a high school English teacher, I had students in my honors classes whose parents chastised them for making an A minus or a B plus. They had to achieve perfection or risk being punished at home. But I also taught students who would, in my non-honors classes, refuse to finish the tests, stating they felt the questions were abstract and irrelevant. In frustration, some students would ball up their papers and exclaim, "The test is stupid. None of this stuff has anything to do with me." They felt the multiple-choice tests focused on extraneous facts disconnected from their real-life experiences and interests.

Testing is not the only cause of their anxiety. Feeling inadequate, trouble fitting in, struggles with weight, appearance and identity, cyber bullying, and many other matters are the crux of frustrations and angst young people feel. Whether or not they are professionally diagnosed as having an anxiety disorder, they do experience inordinate stress at times based on certain triggers that should not be overlooked. An internal pressure cooker of emotions may cause some to have outbursts while others may secretly or silently do harm to themselves or others.

As I was preparing to write this book, I felt strongly that the pervasive negative behaviors of young people were causing them to self-destruct. But I discovered from all the research that it's not the young person; it's the issue, the stressor, that causes their negative behaviors and self-destructive habits. Engaging in drug and alcohol use, bullying or being bullied, premature and unhealthy sexual activity and so many other behaviors actually may be symptoms and outcomes of how various stressors affect youth.

The self-destructive behaviors are how they cope with the stress they feel. In her online article about factors affecting teens, Amy Morin (psychotherapist) identifies these behaviors as depression, bullying, sexual activity, drug use, alcohol abuse, obesity, academic problems, peer pressure, social media and onscreen violence.[6] While stress is not listed as an issue with which they struggle, it certainly is evidence of why many students feel *deflated*.

Despite national initiatives and resources to promote graduation, the dropout rate exceeds more than a million *deflated* students per year. I have learned that, in addition to students who drop out because they just won't do the work necessary to finish school, many drop out for fear they are unable to get into a good college. It's unfortunate that any student would rather drop out of high school than face the possibility of not getting into college. This fear of rejection is a major stressor that limits students' life choices. Many of these students don't know how to work through this fear in a healthy way. The factors Dr. Morin lists may easily lead to or be the result of perpetual miseducation.

Perhaps another, yet paramount, issue that keeps students along with school staff deflated is the occurrence of random, tragic school shootings. This has become perhaps one of the greatest stressors school communities face in the 21st century and yet one of few issues not exacerbated by the pandemic.

On Wednesday, February 14, 2018, I was in Miami, Florida. My husband and I had flown there for a short vacation to visit friends. We were out golfing when we got the news about the shooting at Marjory Stoneman Douglas High School.[7] The nineteen-year-old shooter had entered the school with an automatic rifle and proceeded to shoot and kill seventeen people and wound fifteen more.

That night, we went to the restaurant where we had planned to meet our friends for dinner. One of them is a school leader in Broward County and was at the school that afternoon and well into the evening dealing with the aftermath of the massacre. We were willing to forego our Valentine's Day dinner plans, but his wife said he did not want to cancel. She met us at the restaurant, and we talked as we waited for him to get there.

When he arrived and made his way to our small booth in the back corner, we were at a total loss for words. We knew he had spent all afternoon making sure students were all accounted for and reunited with parents. That is, those who had survived. We explained that we understood if he wanted to just go home. But he had decided he needed something, anything to divert his attention, even momentarily, to something else. So, we bowed our heads while my husband prayed for him, the staff he leads, and the families he serves.

That night was not my first experience consoling a colleague who had dealt with a school shooting so personally. The first was my friend in Denver, an elementary school principal whose two daughters were students at Columbine High School in Littleton, Colorado on April 20, 1999. Two students, ages 18 and 19, shot and killed 13 people, including one teacher, and wounded 26 others.[8]

One of my friend's daughters had left school during lunch, but it had been a couple hours before she could notify her parents of her safety. The other daughter was in the building not far from where shootings occurred. She was held in the auditorium, all afternoon, while my friend waited for hours desperately hoping she'd be invited in to sign for, rather than identify, her child. While she was waiting, I was praying for her, her daughters, and the Columbine community.

To date, there have been over 231 school shootings since Columbine. This has led to national conversations about whether schools should be staffed with armed security officers and teachers. School staff all over the country have been or are being trained on what to do when there is an active shooter on the premises. The trauma and anxiety associated with shootings, drills to respond to shootings, fear of the possibility of shootings and post-traumatic stress of experiencing a shooting all contribute to how emotionally and psychologically deflated students and teachers are feeling.

They are experiencing extraordinary stress and fear daily in their efforts to educate and be educated. Virtual learning has become a more attractive option for parents, teachers, and students, given the COVID19 pandemic. It has heightened stress for educators concerned about contracting the virus during school. It is one of many factors contributing to educators' anxiety. Post pandemic, teachers and school leaders as well as students will need mental health services and personal support.

But they needed this support prior to the pandemic. Difficulty fitting in, death of a loved one, and struggles with weight and identity are not issues isolated to students. Teachers and other school staff deal with these issues, along with that of taking care of a sick child or elderly parent and managing their own chronic illnesses. Many of them are working through a divorce, managing the competing demands of full-time work along with coursework for graduate classes, and even an afterschool job to supplement their income.

They, too, need emotional and psychological support. They need the option of taking a personal leave day to do whatever they choose without judgment. Taking a day to play with their kids, going sailing or fishing, or spending a day shopping or at the spa should not be frowned upon when teachers are entitled to take a personal day to destress. As is the case in professional football, the health and well-being of school staff is a critical component of ensuring readiness and success *on the field*.

HUDDLE UP!
- Provide for students and staff a safe space to discuss their problems and share their personal truth. This is a positive way to boost their confidence and help them cope with life issues.
- Provide appropriate support and personal strategies to both students and staff who are dealing with toxic stress.
- Consider the value and relevance of professional

development related to mindfulness, active listening, and self-care.
- Inform staff and students of safety procedures and protocols in the event of any threatening or potentially harmful occurrence on campus.

CHAPTER TEN
HEADACHES AND CONCUSSIONS

CONCUSSION

A concussion is a traumatic brain injury, usually caused by a blow to the head, that affects your brain function. Effects are usually temporary but can include headaches and problems with concentration, memory, balance, and coordination.

Real Headaches in the Teaching Profession

Endless hours but not enough time. High demands. Low pay. Extensive responsibility. Limited rewards. Many headaches. Teachers are sick and tired of being sick and tired. The teaching profession has too long been viewed as a glorified babysitting job as though they are the ones to keep the kids while the real professionals go to work. But one of the mass discoveries during the pandemic is parents' new understanding of how valuable teachers are and how difficult teaching is. Some parents quickly realized the child they were sending to school was much more of a handful, as a learner, than the child they *thought* they were sending to school.

Perhaps the worst thing a person can say to a teacher is: "You have it made. Your workday ends at 3:30 and you get weekends and summers off." If you ever said this, or even thought it, please stop. Teachers don't have it made. They wish the business world really understood that they, too, have competing projects, stressful deadlines, and some very challenging *clients*.

On any given day of the school year, teachers must serve approximately 25 pre-assigned little *clients*, all at once, in the same meeting space. They are responsible for creating an environment conducive to client success by providing certain terms of agreement, including norms and protocols for client behavior and group interaction. This is called classroom management and cooperative learning. Teachers must willingly hear and kindly respond to every individual client's needs and concerns. This is called building student rapport.

Beyond client meetings, teachers must develop awareness of each individual client's family background, academic history, and learning interests. This is called knowledge of students. The teacher must use this new knowledge to set objectives and identify goals to ensure clients meet certain benchmarks on a learning continuum. This is called strategic planning.

Teachers must provide new meaningful and critical information to all 25 clients, simultaneously, and then differentiate that information to make it more aligned with how clients individually process content. Not only must they differentiate the content but also the methods for how that content is presented. This is effective, differentiated instructional delivery. Teachers must carefully track and quantify the formative and summative progress of clients' mastery of concepts as related to the goals. This is called data-driven decision making or, as in the business world, statistical analysis. In football, it's called player performance analysis.

The teacher must then be able to use the data analysis to determine each client's areas lacking proficiency and then recommend the appropriate one-on-one support for those who have more difficulty understanding various subject matter. This specialized instruction to meet exceptional needs is an important part of the development of an individualized education plan, or IEP. This is called gap analysis and referring special education services.

Even though there is a special education service provider assigned to support some of the clients, it is ultimately the referring teacher who will be held accountable for the extent to which the whole group is able to retain information and perform well on standardized tests. The whole group includes all the clients, despite any inappropriate client behavior, poor attendance, personal trauma, exceptional needs, inability to work with others in the group, and any unwillingness to perform at their best level. This whole-group expectation is important for a teacher's performance-based evaluation, a process used to determine if a teacher is doing a good job.

While all of this is complicated, many teachers do it very well. They are expected to provide these services to all students on the very first day of the job. They are expected to perform well despite lack of adequate mentoring and support, unreasonable supervisors, culturally insensitive colleagues and parents, fear of contracting a virus, and with the not-so-farfetched threat of being shot by an intruder.

At the end of a full day's work, many teachers coach a student athletic team, provide afterschool tutoring, or go to a second job to supplement their income. Of course, they also take care of their families, including children, spouses, and elderly parents. Often at night or early in the morning before work, they grade papers and write lesson plans. For many, a teaching career demands ten to twelve hours a day. Hopefully, endless coffee is available.

Outside the workday, teachers' lives remain, involuntarily and perhaps unfairly, an open book. Anything they say and do may be held against them by the school community. Unlike employees who clock in and out of work, teachers are always on the clock. Whether at church, a restaurant, a movie theater, a grocery store, a bar, or a protest, teachers are always recognized and may be judged. Most students hold their teachers in high regard and everywhere they see them, they do it through the lens of who they are at school.

People who think *teachers have it made* probably know nothing about the accountability, emotional pressure, and competing demands of teaching. But if this is, in fact, what all teachers should know and be able to do, then shouldn't they all have access to the latest technology? Shouldn't they all work in state-of-the-art buildings with access to all the materials and resources they need to be effective? Shouldn't they all be paid at the level of service they provide? Shouldn't they have free or discounted personal childcare options and mental health services? Shouldn't they get the respect and salary they truly deserve? Trying to figure out why the answer to these questions continues to be "not really" is a brain-shaking headache.

Despite the challenges of today's educational system, as related to both working conditions and performance expectations, most teachers across the nation continue to show up every day, in person and online, providing their students with the best instruction and emotional support possible. What others see as hard work, teachers see as *heart work*. To do what they do as well as they do it, under the circumstances in which they do it, is nothing short of amazing. I will never understand why policymakers choose not to give teachers the respect and salary they earn and deserve, and yet consistently demand more of them.

To circumvent a full lesson in brain science and cognitive psychology, I give you this simple explanation. The front part of your brain, the prefrontal cortex, is the region that controls your ability to plan and organize, make personal decisions, and control your behavior and expression. This area of the brain is affected by what teachers know or decide to do as well as what they wish they did not know and don't want to face in the workplace. Trying to manage all the competing priorities of the classroom places great pressure on the prefrontal cortex. In other words, it's a headache.

Dealing with parents can be a headache. Parents often draw conclusions without having all the pertinent details and usually after having not done their part at home. This is not true of all parents, but it is often the case with those who are most vocal. In addition to dealing with parents, teachers must manage relationships with a difficult school leader, seemingly incompetent support personnel, and *that* colleague who is just impossible to work with. These are issues teachers wish they did not have to deal with.

So many teachers and principals can be found at the end of the school day, in a room with the door closed, slumped forward at their desk with their heads down, wondering what to do next and committed to figuring it out. High on their headache list is risk of COVID19 exposure, problems with standardized testing, crowded classrooms, lack of adequate staffing, and student trauma. But that is not all. We must add to this list a national outcry for social justice and the desperate need for school-based anti-racism training. These, too, are issues many teachers and school leaders wish they did not have to deal with.

For me as black woman, it is true that some of my best friends are White. Dr. Richetta, whom I mentioned earlier, is one with whom I have very candid conversations about the headaches she deals with as a school leader and those I deal with as a college professor. We are always grappling with not only how we influence students and their teachers but how we show up for everyone in the broad, diverse communities we serve.

Nothing is *offsides* with us; we hold space for each other to probe hard questions about race. I'm Black, she's White and we are unearthing blackness and unlearning whiteness together. This is how we medicate our social emotional headaches and navigate our way through an often racially charged field of education.

Serious Concussions in the Field of Education

One of the good things about footballs used in the NFL is that they all look the same. No one judges the pigskin for its brown color. There's no choice of a black one or white one. But in the teaching profession, there is certainly a delineation between Black teachers and White teachers. According to the most recent federal report,[1] the workforce of the teaching profession remains close to 80% White, approximately 7% Black, 9% Hispanic, and 2% Asian.

The great divide between blackness and whiteness in schools, especially among staff, is not another headache; it's a concussion. One of the factors that leads to this analogous trauma to the prefrontal cortex is Racial Battle Fatigue (RBF)[2] among teachers of color. Critical race theorist William Smith defines RBF as the interdisciplinary theoretical framework that considers the increased levels of psychosocial stressors and subsequent psychological, physiological, and behavioral responses. RBF is perhaps the biggest headache in the teaching profession for those who are fatigued, that is, and living on the downside of racial disparity.

Smith explains that these RBF responses may include anger, disappointment, resentment, hopelessness, *headache*, backache, and insomnia. This inner battle may also cause teeth grinding, high blood pressure, lack of sleep, withdrawing from social activities, and a dramatic change in diet. You may argue teaching, alone, yields these effects. But Smith asserts that teachers of color exhibit these reactions as a direct result of fighting racial microaggressions throughout the day. The quarterback from the San Francisco 49ers, Colin Kaepernick, was fighting a racial battle as he was scrutinized and outcast when he took a knee against racism.[3]

My first experience with RBF as a teacher was during my first year of teaching. The chair of the high school English department had to intervene on my behalf when the 22-year veteran white male teacher in the room next to mine complained about my classroom management skills. One of my students, who had previously earned bad grades for work he refused to do rather than for inability to do it, got a new attitude when I told him, "If you can memorize the words of Snoop Dogg, you can memorize a poem by Robert Frost, unless, of course, you just don't really know how to rap." My strategy was to provoke him to greatness.

My strategy worked. That Friday afternoon, he brought his boom box to class to play beats along with his hip-hop recitation of Frost's poem, *Stopping Through the Woods on a Snowy Evening*.[4] He did great! It was the first time he memorized a poem, the first time he made an oral presentation in front of all his peers, and the first time he got an A! Throughout his presentation, my students and I were bobbing our heads and following along in the textbook, as he recited every line. We were all so excited for him.

That's when the old man next door rushed in, yelling, "What's going on in here!" When he realized I, too, had joined the party, he reprimanded me in front my students and made all of us "stop this immediately and control yourselves." He reported that I and my students were behaving like animals and that the noise was so loud he thought someone was being attacked. He said it was unprofessional for me to allow students to play rap music in class, and that I had interrupted all the other classes on the hall.

My worse experience with RBF was not in my high school English teacher position but at another education agency for which I worked. I was the only former teacher, the only Black person, and the only doctorate holder on the training team. Colleges seeking to implement culturally responsive practices sought me out specifically, even if they were not in my assigned region. Annoyed that my expertise was in demand, my White colleagues complained that I was "meddling" in their states and talking to clients behind their backs.

When there was no proof of this, they took the "fragile white woman" approach. One cried in a meeting and told everyone I make her feel stupid. Another said she could not focus on her work for worrying I might interfere. She said there were complaints from her clients about me but could not remember specifics. One called my hotel repeatedly, during a trip, asking the staff to confirm I was in my room. My White male supervisor later told me everyone on the team said I was *difficult*.

He began to embarrass me in meetings, commenting that I had changed my hair again, asking why my necklaces "bundled" between my breasts, and announcing I seemed to be gaining weight. He said during my performance review, "Everywhere you go, you are like the emperor with new clothes, thinking you're somebody special, impressing people with your words, while the whole time your rear end is hanging out." (*Rear end* is not the phrase he used.)

I had been warned by Black female colleagues that this would be the treatment as I excelled in my work. "Expect the squeeze; they will make you miserable, trying to force you to quit," they said. I refused to quit. I had anxiety attacks, nightmares, and many repeated headaches. I reported the harassment to the human resources department but that made the environment even worse for me. I was in a constant state of watching my back, being careful what I said or intentionally saying nothing at all. My doctor cried with me, gave me a prescription for migraines, and sent me to a therapist.

I know I speak for other teachers of color when I confess that I have spent far too many days of my career trying to avoid professional conflicts with my White colleagues, trying to get along with those who make it clear they do not want me on the staff, pretending to be grateful as the token Black person allowed to participate on certain teams and committees, and not speaking against the microaggressions related to race and gender in the workplace.

This we-will-get-you-one-way-or-another environment happens at state departments of education, district offices, and local schools. Even in a school building, Black teachers must be aware and concerned about what they say and what they wear, in case it offends someone. We watch our tone in case a fragile White person (colleague, parent, or school leader) feels threatened. We get headaches.

We must convince ourselves the reason we didn't get the job is not because we are Black. We must believe the reason the classroom to which we are assigned, in the far back corner of the building, with no working air-conditioning and no smartboard is not because we are Black. We must convince ourselves the dysfunctional equipment, broken lockers and bathroom doors, limited computers, and unhealthy lunches in the schools where we more often get job placements, is not because we and most of our students are Black. The struggle is real. It's a hard knock against us. We get headaches.

Is structural racism, unconscious bias, and harassment by White counterparts the reason there is a shortage of teachers of color? Perhaps it is. I have my own theories about this. But the fact is, schools need all of us, Black and White. And all students need teachers of color. Therefore, the extent to which licensing exams are a barrier, must be reviewed. Educator preparation programs and ongoing school-based professional development for school staff must include antiracism, cultural responsiveness, restorative engagement, mindfulness, and self-care.

"It Takes All of Us"

Grappling with the disparity in volume of White teachers versus Black teachers as well as students of color versus teachers of color is a real headache. Lack of ethnic minority teachers in high-minority populations is one of the reasons Black and Hispanic children continue to be underserved in many schools. They are not being taught by teachers who share or understand their culture. They are taught and influenced by teachers who may not understand how they live, what their family values are, and how their culture shapes the way they learn.

The heightened social justice battle of 2020, led to the NFL adopting the slogan *End Racism*. Launching a brand campaign entitled *It Takes All of Us*[5] was an effort to promote unity across the country. This was in direct response to police brutality and senseless murders of black men by law enforcement officers who get paid to protect people, not kill people. It was four years after Kaepernick was ousted by the NFL for taking a knee during the singing of the National Anthem as a stand against racial discrimination.

As an adopted Latino raised by White parents, he felt he had to take a stand against the disparity between what we say in America, "one nation under God" and what we do—uphold racist beliefs about inherent differences between people of different races. In 2016, Kaepernick told NFL Media: "I am not going to stand up to show pride in a flag for a country that oppresses Black people and people of color.... this is bigger than football and it would be selfish on my part to look the other way. There are bodies in the street and people getting paid leave and getting away with murder."[6]

Law enforcement agencies as well as schools continue to show evidence of ongoing institutional racism and segregation across America. In the NFL, there are countless health issues, far beyond headaches and migraines, resulting from repeated concussions. This is expected for a high contact, injury laden sport and should be accounted for when negotiating contracts and health insurance plans for active and retired football players, regardless of their race.

From the recent NFL concussion settlement[7] we learn that medical insurance companies were using a "race-norming" formula to support providing different levels of coverage for Black players than for White players. It is important to note that 75 percent of professional football league is Black. Both ethnicities were entitled to coverage for health issues, especially brain damage resulting from concussions. But there was an assumption that a decline in a Black players' brain function is to be expected.

This assumption is a racist belief that "being Black" signifies a lower cognitive function overall, even without playing professional football. Athletes Najeh Davenport and Kevin Henry's legal complaint[8] describes a discriminatory testing regime where doctors can apply different baseline standards; *Black former players have been automatically assumed, through a statistical manipulation called race norming to have started with worse cognitive functioning than white former players.* We must grapple with whether, or the extent to which, "race-norming" also occurs in schools.

Differentiation should be based on what is best for students, not teachers. It should be student-centered, not teacher centered. But this practice of differentiated standards related to race, shows its ugly head both in student performance and teacher licensure data. If the education industry follows the practice of race-norming, then it should be expected that Black teachers and students are outperformed by their White counterparts. The wide disparity in achievement testing results for the past fifty years, for both teachers and students, is persistent.

Should we assume there is nothing irrelevant or culturally insensitive about the tests? Should we conclude, after all these years, the test is always right, and the test-taker is wrong? Do education industry leaders assume people of color are simply less smart than their peers? May we determine this by the test-taker's race, rather than by those who create, score, and analyze the data, and make education policy decisions based upon nationally "normed" criteria?

Is there a biased expectation that White teachers naturally outperform teachers of color, because they may very well be less effective anyway? Do they get more school leadership opportunities because they are naturally better teachers and leaders? Are ethnic minority teachers inherently less intelligent than our counterparts? Do White teachers get better job opportunities, materials, and teaching assistance because they are inherently superior to Black, Indigenous, people of color (BIPOC) teachers? When and where is it safe to raise these questions?

The Proceedings of the National Academics of Science released a publication[9] which indicated that White doctors believe people of color have thicker nerve endings and thicker skin, thus making them (or us) more tolerant of pain. This kind of thinking, an erroneous judgment against humanity, asserts that an entire ethnic group was "built" for abuse. This pain is not limited to the NFL. The effects of racism and unconscious bias are not merely skin deep. Principals, teachers, students, and parents of color all suffer the impact of racial discrimination and battle fatigue.

> Until we engage in substantive change, we will continue to see students and educators experience RBF... Significant work and effort will be required, and as a community of educators, we must move beyond our good intentions and focus on education reform for racial equality.[10]
> —Monika Williams Shealey, Senior Vice President
> Division of Diversity, Equity and Inclusion, Rowan University

---

The NFL's insurance rules were designed based on what is best for them and what keeps money in their pockets as opposed to what is best for the players who are the reason the owners have money in their pockets. Since the NFL is comprised primarily of Black males, then it makes sense there would be more of them suffering concussions and in need of medical assistance in retirement. It makes sense also because more of them are runners and linemen, rather than quarterbacks. The medical insurance benefits should be offered equally to all players on a basis of being on the team, not a basis their race.

As is the case with life-altering discrepancies in services for players on the football field, there are ongoing injustices against players on the education field. Figuratively referred to in this book as headaches and concussions, these discrepancies are serious conditions affecting the health and well-being of both teachers and students. It appears we are not all on the same team with the same goals, resources, access, and opportunities. While it may seem as though we have come a long way in the fight for equity, in many ways we *intentionally* remain separate and unequal.

This matter keeps me up at night because I know we can solve school problems when we really want to. In these dark and deep woods, I concur with Robert Frost: "Whose woods these are, I think I know, ...I have promises to keep, and miles to go before I sleep, and miles to go before I sleep."[11]

HUDDLE UP!

- Celebrate teachers! Acknowledge and celebrate life milestones and accomplishments. Create a school culture that promotes collaboration, positive relationships, and a sense of family.
- Ensure that teachers have adequate resources, access to materials, and a good assistant.
- Encourage teachers to practice self-care and take time off to focus on themselves. Respect their time off as time to be used as they see fit without questioning how they spend that time.
- Acknowledge the layered aspect of a teacher's job description that results in ongoing overlap and competing priorities. Don't mistake or judge a teacher's overall performance based on one small observable segment or moment in time in the classroom.
- Support teacher interactions with parents, as appropriate, and avoid choosing sides when a conflict occurs. Focus on what is best for the student, to find an agreeable solution.
- Use allocated funds to get necessary software and technology devices that will help teachers be more effective. Provide training, resources, and support to

help teachers become adept at using instructional technology.
- Educate both students and teachers on matters of antiracism, unconscious bias, and racial battle fatigue. Provide "safe space" opportunities from them to have professionally facilitated conversations about race, equity, identity, and global consciousness.

CHAPTER ELEVEN
BUILDING THE O-LINE

DELAY OF GAME

A delay of game is a five-yard penalty, which occurs when the O-line (the offensive team) does not put the ball in play before the play clock runs out. Effective school leaders and teachers understand how much is at stake and why every player must be in position and ready to score. They don't waste time on the field.

The offensive line of a football team consists of eleven players who, through good leadership and a series of runs and passes, work the field together, with one goal in mind: getting the ball into the end zone. Of the eleven on the field, five linemen protect the quarterback and block the opponent's defensive team while the other six, who are backs and receivers run and pass the ball until they get it down the field. While it is important to have a defensive line, there are no wins without a skilled and determined "O-line."

The defensive team is the noninstructional staff of a school who has little or no involvement with a school's curriculum but has everything to do with a school's climate and culture. To build a defensive line against blockers of students' academic growth and social-emotional learning, the defensive team in schools must share responsibility for the influence they have on students' safety, well-being and personal choices. They help block opposition that causes pass interferences.

Both the defensive and offensive teams must be good role models because students pay attention to what adults do and don't do. They must listen to students' interests and concerns. They must value what students think and feel, even if they disagree. Students need to know they are seen and heard. Of course, the defensive line must take the lead in protecting the learning environment; that's the purpose of having them. The defensive line of a school staff includes counselors, athletic coaches, custodians, media specialists, and volunteers. They all must advocate for students and their families, equity and inclusion, and restorative justice.

While the defensive line is important for any football team to succeed, it is even more important to develop a strong offensive line of those who are markedly familiar with the end zone and know how to handle the hard hits that come from opponents. Often these opponents are not people; they are standards and policies that work against what is best for students. But when a school has a strong offensive line, teachers are not intimidated by people and policies intended to block them from getting students where they need to be.

I was 22 years old and almost finished with college when I got my first professional teaching job. I say *almost* because I had scarcely finished my student teaching assignment when the principal hired me as a full-time substitute to replace a teacher who was going on medical leave. My mentor teacher was quick to provide a solution when the principal went into full panic mode after receiving news that one of the lead teachers would be out for the rest of the school year. After having supervised me for eight of ten weeks, she strongly recommended that I be brought *on the field*. Of course, I was thrilled for the opportunity.

My mentor, "Mrs. K" was the consummate teaching professional. She had been at the high school for more than twenty years. She held two significant positions *on the field* and in the community—English department chair at the school and Pastor's wife at one of the most prominent churches in the school community. She was highly respected by the players on the field and spectators in the stands.

She was not only my mentor, but she was my first role model for teacher leadership. She modeled school-based problem solving, not only in her role as department chair but also as a staff person who actively supported the principal in his efforts to share leadership. She was neither afraid nor reluctant to disagree with him and she was quick to help him find solutions. Mrs. K recognized me as the solution to the problem.

She played what would be the center position in a football game. The center snaps the ball to the quarterback to start the play. She snapped the ball to the principal, which put the English department's "man down" situation in his hands. But she also provided a strong defense against potential opposition from the school staff and community who normally would not have been receptive to having this 22-year-old college student teaching 18-year-old high school students. Obviously, Ms. K knew how to *neutralize the nose tackle* when the principal *called an audible*. That call was an official pass to me and, fortunately, I understood what wide receivers must do *in the slot*.

"On-the-field heroics will far outweigh any off-field criticism."
—*Terrell Owens, NFL Hall of Fame*

Perhaps another strategy from the principal's playbook could have been to divide the classes and distribute the students evenly among the rest of the English teachers. After all, it was the fourth quarter of the school year. But the better solution and more effective play was to put me on the field. When the principal wasn't sure what to do about the sudden absence of one of the stronger teachers on staff, he and Mrs. K did not delay the game. They huddled up and he figured out what play to call. As a school-based problem solver, she convinced him that I was a good fit for the offensive line, coming off the bench ready to catch a pass and hungry for a touchdown.

One of the reasons some school teams continue to be stuck as they grapple with various challenges throughout the school year is because they are not empowered or experienced in school-based problem-solving. Most of the problems schools face can be solved *on the field* of that school. This is not the athletic field, it's the decision-making table. It's a meeting of master minds. Most of the time, someone on the staff, on the field, has the solution! This is why principals need to lead from the middle and cultivate a strong O-line.

School-based problem-solving requires that starting players are in position and ready to run the play. It also requires they fully understand the expectations of that position and what it takes to play it well. This team of highly skilled, experienced teacher leaders (especially instructional coaches) know what to do on the field, even when the unexpected occurs. Before they go on the field, they already have a plethora of ideas, options, and backup strategies to keep the ball advancing toward the end zone.

When problems arise, the offensive players huddle up to quickly determine a different play, or another strategy. They don't leave the field to go back to the locker room watch other games and wait to see how they address their problems. They devise their own winning game plan based on what works best for them. No matter what problem arises at school there is always an internal solution.

School leaders, which include teachers and principals must sit down before the game starts and determine the right strategy for these students at this time. Together, they build a toolkit and address a myriad of student and staff needs. These include academic performance and effective teaching as well as mental health services for both teachers and students. This demands that the right staff person fulfill the right position and when a change in positioning must happen, staff members are ready and willing to assume the role in which they are most needed.

It is equally important to change and reassign positions when problems occur, as it is to put people in the right positions, initially. Schools need highly skilled team players who are willing to move about and change roles at times to do whatever is best for the team. In a school-based problem-solving culture, teacher leadership teams look out for each other's learning. They share ideas and strategies. They study what effective teams do and what more effectiveness would look like for their school. School-based problem-solving demands that principals open the doors behind which teacher leaders hide and engage them in designing new plays and creating winning strategies for all students, not just those they directly teach.

Touchdowns and interceptions are free game to any change-hungry teacher committed to student success. No one becomes a teacher for fame and glory and certainly not for the money. We teach because schools are failing kids and kids are failing school. We teach because we were born to do it, called to do it and unfulfilled if we can't do it. We approach the P-16 (kindergarten through college) stadium every day, offense and defense, ready to get in the game and score. The focus of the game is to win, and we can't win without making some touchdowns.

Two winning teams walked on the field in Tampa, Florida for Super Bowl LV. The new school team, Kansas City Chiefs, was led by Patrick Lavon Mahomes II, who quit baseball to play football. Effective leaders are focused. While they may be able to do several things, they dedicate themselves to the area wherein they can be most effective. Being focused on what's best and most important is a key leadership attribute of winners.

As the second Black quarterback to win Super Bowl MVP, Mahomes returned to the championship game of the year, having already thrown 114 touchdowns and 24 interceptions. Effective leaders get results. Effective leaders use their influence to help others win, too. In his first season as a starter, he was named NFL Offensive Player of the year and MVP at only 25 years old. Effective leaders show up, no matter how young or new they may be.

The old school team, Tampa Bay Buccaneers, also the home team, was led by 43 year-old Thomas Edward Patrick Brady, Jr., who spent 20 seasons with the New England Patriots. Effective leaders make good decisions, no matter where they go. He has thrown 581 touchdowns and 191 interceptions, with 344 starts in 21 seasons. Effective leaders are committed to continuous improvement.

Brady invited teammate Antonio Brown, wide receiver, to live with him in Tampa, as he had done in New England, to give him time to get acclimated to a new city. Brown and other players speak highly of Brady's influence and camaraderie as their big brother. Effective leaders lift others up because they understand mentorship as the mandate of humanity and the heart of the game. They understand the term "brotherhood" to be more than skin color and bloodlines.

There were two "Patricks" in leadership at Super Bowl LV. Their leadership styles and stats are vastly different, yet both amazing. Both have demonstrated exceptional capacity and expertise to turn a team around. Both of them make good, quick decisions *in the pocket*. What they have most in common is their relentless effort to get to the Super Bowl, their accountability to and responsibility for the teams they lead and the significant impact they have on children.

What school leaders should have in common with them is a relentless commitment to moving their teams forward, accountability and responsibility for the growth or the staff and students they lead and serve, and dedication to making a lasting impact on the lives of children whose learning is at stake. Above all, school leaders must know how to win.

"...*Tom's* preparation was unbelievable, just his confidence and how it rubs off on the rest of the football team. Talking to defensive players, he might see something on tape and give a heads up. ...His leadership is off the charts. ...He protects the football so well in big games and we have very few turnovers. He's a winner and that's all you can say. He brought a winning mentality to a really talented football team that didn't know how to win."
—*Bruce Arians, Buccaneers' Head Coach*[1]

WHY SCHOOLS FUMBLE

It is interesting to hear Coach Arians say he had a talented team he felt did not know how to win. Why couldn't he and his assistant coaches teach them how? Did they as leaders have a defeated mindset. Is talent not enough for the challenges his team faced? I see this phenomenon in schools all the time. Principals and teachers say they know their talented teams can do it but, for some reason, they aren't getting it done. The principal often cannot articulate what the "some reason" is.

When I work closely with them, it becomes clear they really don't know the reason why they aren't getting the intended outcomes. But talent is usually a non-issue. Team talent means nothing if it is not utilized and cultivated in a way that generates results. Most school teams aren't lacking in talent. They lack strategic appropriation of talent. They lack leadership necessary to put each person on the staff in the position that best fits their talent.

Sometimes talent is confused with time. Just because a player has been on the team a long time does not mean that player is effective on the field. Educators must stop valuing seniority over effectiveness. Talent must be evidenced by effective performance, not longevity. Everyone on the school team must be held accountable for high performance outcomes. They must be willing to periodically accept assignments in which they may perform at a higher capacity, even when it is not their preferred role. Assigning instructional staff to teach classes and subjects they want to teach, rather than where they are most needed, is one of the main reasons why schools aren't getting the best results.

Celebrating talent for the sake of having it rather than for results produced from it is another reason. Why reward talent if it's not a game changer? Who cares how much a teacher loves teaching third grade and loves her third graders if after several weeks of school, there remains little or no evidence of academic progress? Teaching ability must be matched with intended outcomes for student learning. Instructional capacity is the leading indicator of an effective teacher. What teachers know and are able to do is the most important component of school improvement.

No Superbowl game was ever won without grit and rigor. My students said they had a love-hate relationship with me when I was a high school English teacher. They said they loved me as a teacher but hated the hard work. But hard work pays off. School improvement plans must include the hard work that needs to be done, a clear plan for how to get it done, and who on the staff will take the lead or make the changes necessary for fully implementing reform.

Somehow school reform has become a dirty word. School leaders and teacher leaders don't like to use it,. They say school does not need to be reformed. Yes, it does! Part of the reason Brady was welcomed by the Buccaneers was because the whole team, not just Coach Arians and team owners, knew they needed a change, a big change. The game plan had to be reformed. Some roles had to change. Some had to leave the team and others needed to join. Marginal players had to level up or be left on the sidelines. Real change often demands radical reform.

The truth is, there were missing pieces in the leadership's game plan. I'm sure they had a plan, but obviously all the pieces weren't coming together. Coach Arians, he probably had vision, objectives, core values, and strategy. What he needed was a strong team leader who knew how to translate the ideas in the playbook to outcome-based activity on the field. This is where a veteran quarterback and master teacher like Tom Brady, makes the difference.

Regardless of how anyone feels about Brady's football legacy and the teams he has served, his results speak for themselves. Seven Superbowl wins with almost 600 touchdown passes is the record of a GOAT. Results like these are the markings of great team leadership. But Brady has had controversy. Terrell Owens has, too. But he is undeniably a game changer. His ranks third in his career as wide receiver, with 153 touchdowns. One doesn't have to be perfect to lead. All leaders make mistakes.

But again, effectiveness is defined by results. Schools need effective, strategic-thinking leaders and leadership teams. It's not that Brady, alone, made the team a winning team. Brady helped the team implement Arians' plan with fidelity. Together, they were able to devise a plan and see it all the way through. Unfortunately, the inability to fully implement plans and programs schoolwide continues to be a big problem in the education field.

There are so many lessons the education community can learn from Super Bowl LV. The Chiefs were missing two starting offensive tackles. Lesson one: *You can't make touchdowns when your key players are not on the field.* Their quarterback came on the field with an injury. Lesson two: *You can't lead well or perform at high capacity when you don't feel well.* Their quarterback was pressured for more than half of his drop backs. Lesson three: *School leaders need a strong support system among staff in order to affect change.* The Buccaneers completely shut down the Chiefs' leading wide receiver. Lesson four: *You can't move student learning forward when you allow ongoing interferences that hinder teachers from doing their best work.* The Chiefs approached the Superbowl LV as reigning champions, having won Superbowl LIV with a 31 to 21 score, in addition to a 12 to 4 season record. And above all, Lesson five: *What worked last year may not work this year.* Last year's data does not determine this year's win.

Each year, school leadership teams must huddle up to determine what new plays to make, new strategies to employ and who to place in new positions. The stakes are high for school communities. Black and brown children do not have teachers who look like them. Standardized tests continue to create a great divide between the haves and the have nots. Parents and families aren't sure where their next meal is coming from. Students are bullying and being bullied. While some teens are carelessly bringing lives into the world, others are carefully contemplating suicide.

The weight of the pandemic and the challenges of virtual learning has had a grave impact on educators well as students and their families. Students with exceptional needs continue to be the most disadvantaged. Athletes who felt their destiny hinges on their ability to get sports scholarships are uncertain about the future. High schoolers who have looked forward to the parties, prom and graduation were forced to resort to sidewalk celebrations, birthday drive-bys and online ceremonies.

New and novice teachers quickly adjusted to the virtual demands of teaching but often without the mentoring and professional development necessary to expand their instructional skills. Some veteran teachers who were not as astute in instructional technology struggled to engage and relate to students through a virtual learning platform. Many were concerned about not only the pre-existing conditions of family members but that of their own. Some teachers are voluntarily leaving the teaching profession while others have been laid off or were forced to leave due to a sick family member or their own sheer burnout.

The teacher shortage is increasing. School leaders may have to bring a *Gronk* (Robert Gronkowski) out of retirement to win. They may have to get an *AB* (Antonio Brown), a free agent who can excel in more than one position on the field and guarantee the end zone. Or, they may have to move a Leonard Fournette, to the right place and then create space for a JPP (Jason Pierre-Paul) to prove he still has what it takes, even after a hand injury. These changes worked for the Buccaneers once they assessed what was not working and why.

Despite adversity, standardized testing, and a pandemic, school leaders must declare this is not the time to fumble! We can create environments where all students can and do learn. Once we understand several of the reasons *why* schools fumble, we can focus our attention on providing school leaders with the right support to prevent fumbling. No one intentionally fumbles the ball. If a fumble occurs, something has gone wrong.

As a team of strategic thinkers and leaders, we can assess what is going wrong and why. We can use assessment results to determine what it takes to win. Let's think and work together to strengthen the offensive line so we can do whatever it takes to get more children into the end zone. As I always say: *When we think together, we think better, and that is how we accomplish what we, alone, thought we could not do.* So, huddle up! Let us not delay the game.

"At some point during the course of the game, I will have an impact—whether it's blocking or whether it's catching the football. I will do whatever it takes to win."
—Terrell Owens, NFL Hall of Fame

ABOUT THE AUTHOR

Dr. Cathy Owens Oliver, #DrCathyO, is a speaker, author, professor, instructional leadership coach, education policy analyst, school board member, and National Board Certified Teacher. CEO of Educational Effectiveness Group, she helps education agencies develop school leaders, increase teacher readiness, transform school culture, and close the equity gap.

Having more than 25 years of service, she has worked with state education officials in 46 of 50 states and in Canada coaching teachers, school leaders, boards of education, and college faculty. Formerly a high school English teacher, she has worked for the NC Department of Public Instruction, the Michigan Association of Independent School Administrators, the National Board for Professional Teaching Standards, Learning Forward, and Educational Testing Service.

She has presented at countless national conferences and written for leading education journals including *Accomplished Teacher Magazine*, the *Journal of Staff Development*, and the Hope Foundation's *What Works in Schools* newsletter. Her work also appears in the college textbook: *Black Star: An Introduction to African American Studies*.

She completed undergraduate studies at the University of NC at Greensboro and postgraduate studies at NC A&T State University and Seton Hall University where she earned her doctorate in Education, Leadership, Management, and Policy. She is the Dean of Education for the COGIC International Sunday School Department and member of the Publishing Board.

www.drcathyo.com
www.edueffectiveness.com

REFERENCES

Acosta, JP. (2021, June 25). *The NFL's Concussion Settlement Marginalizes Black Athletes.* SBNation. https://www.sbnation.-com/nfl/2021/6/25/22550879/nfl-race-norming-concussion-settlement

Adelson, E. (2020). QB Chaos. *Athlon Sports Pro Football Preview.*

American Bar Association. (2001, February). *School Discipline Zero Tolerance Policies.* https://www.americanbar.org/groups/public_interest/child_law/resources/attorneys/school_disciplinezerotolerancepolicies/

Anderson, M., & Jiang, J. (2020, August 28). *Teens' Social Media Habits and Experiences.* Pew Research Center: Internet, Science & Tech. https://www.pewresearch.org/internet/2018/11/28/teens-social-media-habits-and-experiences/.

Arians, B. (2021, February 7). NFL Prime Time.

Asher, J. (2017). *Thirteen Reasons Why.* Penguin Young Readers Group.

REFERENCES

Ayers, W. (1993). *To teach: the journey of a teacher*. New York: Teachers College Press.

Ben. (2017, December 20). A Brief History of the SAT and How It Changes [web log]. https://www.petersons.com/blog/a-brief-history-of-the-sat-and-how-it-changes/.

Boser, U. (2011). (rep.). *Teacher Diversity Matters: A State-by-State Analysis of Teachers of Color*. Center for American Progress. Retrieved from https://www.americanprogress.org/issues/education-k-12/reports/2011/11/09/10657 teacher-diversity-matters/.

Boston Regional Office., The effects of coaching on standardized admission examinations: staff memorandum of the Boston Regional Office of the Federal Trade Commission (1979). Boston; Federal Trade Commission.

Boyd, D., Goldhaber, D., Lankford, H. & Wycoff, J. (2007). The Effect of Certification and Preparation on Teacher Quality. Future Child, 17(1), 45-68. https://files.eric.ed.gov/fulltext/EJ795877.pdf.

Burke-Harris, N. (2018). *The Deepest Well: Healing the Long-Term Effects of Childhood Adversity*. Houghton Mifflin Harcourt.

Centers for Disease Control, (2019). *Many Young People Engage in Sexual Risk*. National Youth Risk Behavior Survey. https://www.cdc.gov/healthyyouth/data/yrbs/pdf/trendsreport.pdf

"Child Sexual Abuse Statistics," National Center for Victims of Crime. https://victimsofcrime.org/child-sexual-abuse-statistics/

Columbine High School Massacre. (2021, May 2). In *Wikipedia*. https://en.wikipedia.org/wiki/Columbine_High_School_massacre

Crouse, K. (2007, January 23). *Bears Coach Smith Reflects on His Roots*. The New York Times.

The College Board. (2018, October 25). *SAT Suite of Assessments Annual Reports*. SAT Suite Program Results: 2017.

REFERENCES

https://reports.collegeboard.org/pdf/2017-total-group-sat-suite-assessments-annual-report.pdf.

The College Board. (2020, September 9). *Nearly 2.2 Million Students in the Class of 2020 Took The SAT At Least Once.* Newsroom. https://newsroom.collegeboard.org/nearly-22-million-students-class-2020-took-sat-least-once.

Dale, M. (2020, August 25). Lawyers: NFL concussion awards discriminate Against Blacks. WashingtonPost. https://www.washingtonpost.-com/health/lawyers-nfl-concussion-awards-discriminate-against-blacks/2020/08/25/7caa3454-e718-11eabf44-0d31c85838a5_sto-ry.html

Fox 2000 Pictures. (2017). Hidden Figures. Fox 2000 Pictures.

Freiberg, H. (1999). *School climate: Measuring, improving and sustaining healthy learning environment. Palmer Press.*

Frost, R. "Stopping by Woods on a Snowy Evening." *Collected Poems, Prose, & Plays.* Library of America.

Gadsden, V. (2010). *Father Involvement and Early Childhood Development. Addressing Achievement Gap Symposium.* Princeton; NJ.

Gardner, K. (2014, November). Should Schools or Judges Decide School Policies? *Law Wise.*

Kansas Bar Association. 3. https://cdn.ymaws.com/www.ksbar.org/resource/collection/F729F565-5794-47F9-BD7210AEC1A908DA/LW1411.pdf

Gillespie, N. (2015). A Short, Sad History of Zero-Tolerance School Policies. *Reason Magazine.* https://reason.-com/2015/10/05/a-short-sad-history-of-zero-tolerance-sc/

Hamm, M., Newton A. & Chisholm. (2015). A. Prevalence and Effect of Cyberbullying on Children and Young People: A scoping

REFERENCES

review of social media studies. *JAMA Pediatrics.* 169(8):770–777. doi:10.1001/jamapediatrics.2015.0944.

Hanushek, E., Peterson, P., Talpey, L., & Woessmann, L. (2019). The Achievement Gap Fails to Close: Half Century of Testing Shows Persistent Divide between Haves and Have-Nots. *Education Next,* 19(3), 8–17. https://doi.org/http://hanushek.stanford.edu/publications/achievement-gap-fails-close-half-century-testing-shows-persistent-divide-between-haves

Hickling, M. (2005). *The new speaking of sex: what your children need to know and when they need to know it.* Northstone Publishing.

Hood, R. (2019, March 6). *Very Interesting Conversation With a 10th Grader.* https://www.facebook.com/groups/principalprinciplesleadership/

Hoffman, K., Trawalter, S., Axt, J., & Oliver, M. (2016.) *Racial bias in pain assessment.* Proceedings of the National Academy of Sciences, 113 (16) 4296 4301; DOI: 10.1073/pnas.1516047113 https://www.pnas.org/content/113/16/4296/tab-figures-data

Horton, A. (2019, April 13). *Suspected Parkland gunman pens love letters about fathering children - and naming them after guns.* The Washington Post. https://www.washingtonpost.com/nation/2019/04/09/suspected-parkland-gunman-pens-love-letters-about-fathering-children-naming-them-after-guns/.

Hunt, M., Marx, R., Lipson, C., & Young, J. (2018). Author Index to Volume 37, 2018. *Journal of Social and Clinical Psychology,* 37(10), 835–840. https://doi.org/10.1521/jscp.2018.37.10.835

Irvine, J. (1990). *Black students and school failure: policies, practices, and prescriptions.* New York: Greenwood Press.

REFERENCES

Iruka, I. U. (2016). State Policy and Research for Early Education Working Group. In *National Conference of State Legislators*. Chicago, IL; NCSL.org.

Kendi, I. X. (2016). Why the Academic Achievement Gap Is a Racist Idea. *Black Perspectives*. https://doi.org/African American Intellectual Historical Society

Kendrick Brothers Productions. (2015, December 22). War Room (DVD). United States.

Knapp, M., & Shields, P. (1990). Reconceiving Academic Instruction for the Children of Poverty. *Pi Delta Kappan, 71*(10), 752–758. https://doi.org/http://www.jstor.org/stable/20404280

Koehler, A. (2020, December 8). *Baby, it's cold outside: How cold temps affect NFL games*. USA Today. https://touchdownwire.usatoday.com/lists/nfl-cold-temperatures-affect-games-2020/.

Kohn, A. (2000). *The Case Against Standardized Testing: Raising the Scores, Ruining the Schools*. Heinemann.

Kraft, M. A., & Gilmour, A. F. (2017). Revisiting The Widget Effect: Teacher Evaluation Reforms and the Distribution of Teacher Effectiveness. *Educational Researcher, 46*(5), 234–249. https://doi.org/10.3102/0013189x17718797

Ladson-Billings, G. (1994). *The Dreamkeepers: Successful Teaching for African-American Students*. Josey-Bass.

McGillivray, N. (2014, January 15). *What Are the Effects of Social Media on Youth?* TurboFuture. https://turbofuture.com/internet/effects-of-social-media-on-our-youth.

McMahon, P. (2018, February 17). *Nikolas Cruz: 'We had this monster living under our roof and we didn't know.'*. Sun Sentinel. https://www.sun-sentinel.com/local/broward/parkland/florida-school-shooting/fl-school-shooting-family-helped-nikolas-cruz-20180217-story.html.

Medina, J., Benner, K., & Taylor, K. (2019, March

REFERENCES

12). *Actresses, Business Leaders and Other Wealthy Parents Charged in U.S. College Entry Fraud.* The New York Times. https://www.nytimes.com/2019/03/12/us/college-admissions-cheating-scandal.html.

Menzer, J. (2020). Q&A with Christian McCaffrey. *Athlon Sports Pro Football Preview.*

Morin, A. (2020, June 24). *The Top 10 Social Issues Teens Face in the Digital World.* Verywell Family. https://www.verywellfamily.com/startling-facts-about-todays-teenagers-2608914.

National Board for Professional Teaching Standards. *Overview: National Board Certification.* https://www.nbpts.org/national-board-certification/.

National Football League. *NFL launches season-long brand campaign 'It Takes All of Us'.* (2020, September), www.NFL.com. https://www.nfl.com/news/nfl-launches-season-long-brand-campaign-it-takes-all-of-us

Neufeld, S. (2013, June 27). *Addressing the Achievement Gap: The Earliest Intervention.* The Atlantic. https://www.theatlantic.com/national/archive/2013/06/addressing-the-achievement-gap-the-earliest-intervention/277141/.

Office of Elementary and Secondary Education, State plans to ensure equitable access to excellent educators (2015). Washington, DC; USDOE. https://www2.ed.gov/programs/titleiparta/equitable/eafaq2015.pdf

OWN. (2017, September 2). Oprah's Masterclass. *Steve Harvey.* episode.

Rabin, C., Teproff, C., Herrara, C. & Smiley, D. (2018, February 15). *A Detestable Act.* Miami Herald.

Shealey, M. (2020, September 21). Overcoming Racial Battle

REFERENCES

Fatigue Through Education Reform [web log]. https://edprepmatters.net/2020/09/overcoming-racial-battle-fatigue-through-education-reform/.

Sheehan, S. (2020, May 11). *Tom Brady Defied Bill Belichick's Refusal to Draft Premium Weapons.* Sportscasting.com. https://www.sportscasting.com/tom-brady-defied-bill-belichicks-refusal-to-draft-premium-weapons/.

Sifferlin, A. (2016, June). Stress Is Contagious in the Classroom. *Time Magazine.*

Simmons, M. (2015, November 16). Many Blame Big Corporation, Pearson, for School Testing Malaise. *Maryland Reporter.* https://marylandreporter.com/2020/03/10/emergency-legislation-aims-to-increase-access-to-health-care-in-state-of-emergency/.

Smart Social. (2020, February 25). *Teen Social Media Statistics 2018 (What Parents Need to Know).* Smart Social. https://smartsocial.com/social-media-statistics/.

Smith, W. David, R., & Stanton, G.S. (2020). Racial Battle Fatigue: The Long-Term Effects of Racial Microaggressions on African American Boys and Men, Majors, R., Carberry,

K. and Ransaw, T. (ed.) *The International Handbook of Black Community Mental Health.* Emerald Publishing Limited, Bingley,83-92. https://doi.org/10.1108/978-1-83909-964-920201006

Taie, S., & Goldring, R. (2020). Characteristics of Public and Private Elementary and Secondary School Teachers in the United States: Results From the 2017–18 National Teacher and Principal Survey First Look (NCES 2020- 142). U.S. Department of Education. Washington, DC: National Center for Education Statistics. https://nces.ed.gov/pubsearch/pubsinfo.asp?pubid=2020142.

REFERENCES

Taylor, V. J., & Walton, G. M. (2011). Stereotype Threat Under-mines Academic Learning. *Personality and Social Psychology Bulletin,* 37(8), 1055–1067. https://doi.org/10.1177/0146167211406506

Thomas, J. (2018, February 4). *Super Bowl 2018 Final Score for Eagles vs. Patriots: Eagles Fought Like Hell to Win Their First Super Bowl.* SBNation. https://www.sbnation.com/2018/2/4/16971908/patriots-eagles-2018-super-bowl-52-results-final-score.

Thomas Nelson, Inc. (1976). *King James Bible,* 2 Samuel 4:4.

U.S. Department of Education, Office of Elementary and Secondary Education (2015). *State plans to ensure equitable access to excellent educators.* https://www2.ed.gov/programs/titleiparta/equitable/eafaq2015.pdf

Weisberg, D., Sexon, S., Mulhern, J., & Publication, D. (2009). (rep.). *The Widget Effect: Our National Failure to Acknowledge and Act on Differences in Teacher Effectiveness.* 2nd ed. Brooklyn, NY: The New Teacher Project (TNTP). https://tntp.org/publications/view/the-widget-effect-failure-to-act-on-differences-in-teacher-effectiveness

Wilkinson, s. (2019, August 13). *Back to School by the Numbers: 2019-20 School Year.* NCES. https://nces.ed.gov/blogs/nces/post/back-to-school-by-the-numbers-2019-20-school-year.

Williams, C. (2020). 16 Things to Watch in 2020. *Athlon Sports Pro Football Preview.*

Williams, W., Adrien, R., Murthy, C. & Pietryka, D. (2016). *Equitable access to excellent ducators: An analysis of states' educator equity plans.* Westat. https://www2.ed.gov/programs/titleiparta/equitable/titleiiequity-analysis1031.pdf

REFERENCES

Wyche, S. (2016, August 27). Colin Kaepernick Explains Why He Sat During the NationalAnthem. *NFL.com*. https://www.nfl.com/news/colin-kaepernick-explains-why-he-sat-during-national-anthem-0ap3000000691077

FOOTNOTES

Introduction

1. Wilkinson, S. (2019, August 13). *Back to School by the Numbers: 2019-20 School Year*. NCES. https://nces.ed.gov/blogs/nces/post/ back-to-school-by-the-numbers-2019-20-school-year

Chapter One

1. Thomas, J. (2018, February 4). *Super Bowl 2018 Final Score for Eagles vs. Patriots: Eagles Fought Like Hell to Win Their First Super Bowl*. SBNation. https://www.sbnation.com/ 2018/2/4/16971908/patriots-eagles-2018-super-bowl-52-results-final-score.
2. Adelson, E. "NFL Q Adelson, E. (2020). QB Chaos. *Athlon Sports Pro Football Preview*.
3. Crouse, K. (2007, January 23). *Bears Coach Smith Reflects on His Roots*. The New York Times.
4. Menzer, J. (2020). Q&A with Christian McCaffrey. *Athlon Sports Pro Football Preview*.
5. Williams, C. (2020). 16 Things to Watch in 2020. *Athlon Sports Pro Football Preview*.

Chapter Three

1. Boyd, D., Goldhaber, D., Lankford, H. & Wycoff, J. (2007). The Effect of Certification and Preparation on Teacher Quality. *Future Child*, 17(1), 45-68. https://files.eric.ed.gov/fulltext/EJ795877.pdf.
2. U.S. Department of Education, Office of Elementary and Secondary Education (2015). *State plans to ensure equitable access to excellent educators*. https://www2.ed.gov/programs/titleiparta/equitable/eafaq2015.pdf
3. Weisberg, D., Sexon, S., Mulhern, J., & Publication, D. (2009). (rep.). *The Widget Effect: Our National Failure to Acknowledge and Act on Differences in Teacher Effectiveness*. 2nd ed. Brooklyn, NY: The New Teacher Project

(TNTP). https://tntp.org/ publications/view/the-widget-effect-failure-to-act-on-differences-in-teacher-effectiveness

4. Kraft, M. A., & Gilmour, A. F. (2017). Revisiting The Widget Effect: Teacher Evaluation Reforms and the Distribution of Teacher Effectiveness. *Educational Researcher*, 46(5), 234–249. https://doi.org/10.3102/0013189x17718797

5. Sheehan, S. (2020, May 11). *Tom Brady Defied Bill Belichick's Refusal to Draft Premium Weapons*. Sportscasting.com. https://www.sportscasting.com/tom-brady-defied-bill-belichicks-refusal-to-draft-premium-weapons/.

Chapter Four

1. Iruka, I. U. (2016). State Policy and Research for Early Education Working Group. In *National Conference of State Legislators*. Chicago, IL; NCSL.org.
2. Neufeld, S. (2013, June 27). *Addressing the Achievement Gap: The Earliest Intervention*. The Atlantic. https://www.theatlantic.com/national/archive/2013/06/addressing-the-achievement-gap-the-earliest-intervention/277141/.
3. Kohn, A. (2000). *The Case Against Standardized Testing: Raising the Scores, Ruining the Schools*. Heinemann.
4. Simmons, M. (2015, November 16). Many Blame Big Corporation, Pearson, for School Testing Malaise. *Maryland Reporter*. https://marylandreporter.com/2020/03/10/emergency-legislation-aims-to-increase-access-to-health-care-in-state-of-emergency/.
5. Kohn, A. (2000). *The Case Against Standardized Testing: Raising the Scores, Ruining the Schools*. Heinemann.
6. Ben. (2017, December 20). A Brief History of the SAT and How It Changes [web log]. https://www.petersons.com/blog/a-brief-history-of-the-sat-and-how-it-changes/.
7. Boston Regional Office., The effects of coaching on standardized admission examinations: staff memorandum of the Boston Regional Office of the Federal Trade Commission (1979). Boston; Federal Trade Commission.
8. The College Board. (2018, October 25). *SAT Suite of Assessments Annual Reports*. SAT Suite Program Results: 2017. https://reports.collegeboard.org/pdf/2017-total-group-sat-suite-assessments-annual-report.pdf.
9. College Board, Nearly 2.2 Million Students in the Class of 2020, 2020. The College Board. (2020, September 9). *Nearly 2.2 Million Students in the Class of 2020 Took The SAT At Least Once*. Newsroom. https://newsroom.collegeboard.org/nearly-22-million-students-class-2020-took-sat-least-once.
10. Medina, J., Benner, K., & Taylor, K. (2019, March 12). *Actresses, Business Leaders and Other Wealthy Parents Charged in U.S. College Entry Fraud*. The

FOOTNOTES

New York Times. https://www.nytimes.com/2019/03/12/us/college-admissions-cheating-scandal.html.
11. Ayers, W. (1993). *To teach: the journey of a teacher.* New York: Teachers College Press.
12. Taylor, V. J., & Walton, G. M. (2011). Stereotype Threat Undermines Academic Learning. *Personality and Social Psychology Bulletin,* 37(8), 1055–1067. https://doi.org/10.1177/0146167211406506
13. Kendi, I. X. (2016). Why the Academic Achievement Gap Is a Racist Idea. *Black Perspectives.* https://doi.org/African American Intellectual Historical Society
14. See Kendi, I.X. (2016)
15. Hanushek, E., Peterson, P., Talpey, L., & Woessmann, L. (2019). The Achievement Gap Fails to Close: Half Century of Testing Shows Persistent Divide between Haves and Have-Nots. *Education Next, 19*(3), 8–17. https://doi.org/http://hanushek.stanford.edu/

Chapter Five

1. Gadsden, V. (2010). *Father Involvement and Early Childhood Development. Addressing Achievement Gap Symposium.* Princeton; NJ.
2. Kendrick Brothers Productions. (2015, December 22). War Room (DVD). United States.
3. McMahon, P. (2018, February 17). *Nikolas Cruz: 'We had this monster living under our roof and we didn't know.'.* Sun Sentinel. https://www.sun-sentinel.com/local/broward/parkland/florida-school-shooting/fl-school-shooting-family-helped-nikolas-cruz-20180217-story.html.
4. Horton, A. (2019, April 13). *Suspected Parkland gunman pens love letters about fathering children - and naming them after guns.* The Washington Post. https://www.washingtonpost.com/nation/2019/04/09/suspected-parkland-gunman-pens-love-letters-about-fathering-children-naming-them-after-guns/.
5. Thomas Nelson, Inc. (1976). *King James Bible,* 2 Samuel 4:4.
6. OWN. (2017, September 2). Oprah's Masterclass. *Steve Harvey.* Episode 6.

Chapter Six (Epigraph)

1. Koehler, A. (2020, December 8). *Baby, it's cold outside: How cold temps affect NFL games.* USA Today. https://touchdownwire.usatoday.com/lists/nfl-cold-temperatures-affect-games-

FOOTNOTES

Chapter Six

1. Freiberg, H. (1999). *School climate: Measuring, improving and sustaining healthy learning environment.* Palmer Press.
2. Anderson, M., & Jiang, J. (2020, August 28). *Teens' Social Media Habits and Experiences.* Pew Research Center: Internet, Science & Tech. https://www.pewresearch.org/internet/2018/11/28/teens-social-media-habits-and-experiences/.
3. Morin, A. (2020, June 24). *The Top 10 Social Issues Teens Face in the Digital World.* Verywell Family. https://www.verywellfamily.com/startling-facts-about-todays-teenagers-2608914.
4. Fox 2000 Pictures. (2017) Hidden Figures. Fox 2000 Pictures.
5. McGillivray, N. "What Are the Effects of Social Media on Youth?" TurboFuture, January 15, 2014. https://turbofuture.com/internet/effects-of-social-media-on-our-youth.
6. Hunt, M., Marx, R., Lipson, C., & Young, J. (2018). Author Index to Volume 37, 2018. *Journal of Social and Clinical Psychology,* 37(10), 835–840. https://doi.org/10.1521/jscp.2018.37.10.835
7. Smart Social. (2020, February 25). *Teen Social Media Statistics 2018 (What Parents Need to Know).* Smart Social. https://smartsocial.com/social-media-statistics/.
8. Hamm, M., Newton A. & Chisholm. (2015). A. Prevalence and Effect of Cyberbullying on Children and Young People: A scoping review of social media studies. JAMA Pediatrics. 169(8):770–777. doi:10.1001/jamapediatrics.2015.0944.

Chapter Seven

1. "Child Sexual Abuse Statistics," National Center for Victims of Crime. https://victimsofcrime.org/child-sexual-abuse-statistics/
2. Hickling, M. (2005). *The new speaking of sex: what your children need to know and when they need to know it.* Northstone Publishing.
3. Centers for Disease Control, (2019). *Many Young People Engage in Sexual Risk.* National Youth Risk Behavior Survey. https://www.cdc.gov/healthyyouth/data/yrbs/pdf/trendsreport.pdf
4. See Centers for Disease Control, (2019).

FOOTNOTES

Chapter Eight

1. American Bar Association. (2001, February). *School Discipline Zero Tolerance Policies.* https://www.americanbar.org/groups/public_interest/child_law/resources/attorneys/school_disciplinezerotolerancepolicies/
2. Gillespie, N. (2015). A Short, Sad History of Zero-Tolerance School Policies. *Reason Magazine.* https://reason.com/2015/10/05/a-short-sad-history-of-zero-tolerance-sc/
3. See Gillespie. N. (2015)
4. Institute for Education Sciences. (2020, December). Now Is the Time for Teachers to Use Data-Based Inquiry Cycles [web log]. https://ies.ed.gov/ncee/edlabs/regions/west/Blogs/Details/25.
5. Irvine, J. (1990). *Black students and school failure: policies, practices, and prescriptions.* New York: Greenwood Press.
6. Overview: National Board for Professional Teaching Standards. *Overview: National Board Certification.* https://www.nbpts.org/national-board-certification/.

Chapter Nine

1. Hood, R. (2019, March 6). *Very Interesting Conversation With a 10th Grader.*https://www.facebook.com/groups/principalprinciplesleadership/
2. Asher, J. (2017). *Thirteen Reasons Why.* Penguin Young Readers Group.
3. Burke-Harris, N. (2018). *The Deepest Well: Healing the Long-Term Effects of Childhood Adversity.* Houghton Mifflin Harcourt.
4. Sifferlin, A. (2016, June). Stress Is Contagious in the Classroom. *Time Magazine.*
5. See Kohn, A. (2000)
6. Morin, A. (2020, June 24). *The Top 10 Social Issues Teens Face in the Digital World.* Verywell Family. https://www.verywellfamily.com/startling-facts-about-todays-teenagers-2608914.
7. Rabin, C., Teproff, C., Herrara, C. & Smiley, D. (2018, February 15). *A Detestable Act.* Miami Herald.
8. Wikipedia. 2020. Columbine High School Massacre. (2021, May 2). In *Wikipedia.* https://en.wikipedia.org/wiki/Columbine_High_School_massacre

Chapter Ten

1. Taie, S., & Goldring, R. (2020). Characteristics of Public and Private Elementary and Secondary School Teachers in the United States: Results.
2. Smith, W. David, R., & Stanton, G.S. (2020). Racial Battle Fatigue: The Long-Term Effects of Racial Microaggressions on African American Boys and Men, Majors, R., Carberry, K. and Ransaw, T. (ed.) *The International Handbook of Black Community Mental Health.* Emerald Publishing Limited, Bingley, 83-92. https://doi.org/10.1108/978-1-83909-964-920201006
3. Wyche, S. (2016, August 27). Colin Kaepernick Explains Why He Sat During the National Anthem. *NFL.com*. https://www.nfl.com/news/colin-kaepernick-explains-why-he-sat-during-national-anthem-0ap3000000691077
4. Frost, R. "Stopping by Woods on a Snowy Evening." *Collected Poems, Prose, & Plays*. Library of America.
5. National Football League. *NFL launches season-long brand campaign 'It Takes All of Us'.* (2020, September), www.NFL.com. https://www.nfl.com/news/nfl-launches-season-long-brand-campaign-it-takes-all-of-us
6. Wyche, S. (2016, August 27). Colin Kaepernick Explains Why He Sat During the National Anthem. *NFL.com*.
7. Acosta, JP. (2021, June 25). *The NFL's Concussion Settlement Marginalizes Black Athletes.* SBNation. https://www.sbnation.com/nfl/2021/6/25/22550879/nfl-race-norming-concussion-settlement
8. Dale, M. (2020, August 25). Lawyers: NFL concussion awards discriminate Against Blacks. Washington Post. https://www.washingtonpost.com/health/lawyers-nfl-concussion-awards-discriminate-against-blacks/2020/08/25/7caa3454-e718-11ea-bf44-0d31c85838a5_story.html
9. Hoffman Hoffman, K., Trawalter, S., Axt, J., & Oliver, M. (2016.) *Racial bias in pain assessment.* Proceedings of the National Academy of Sciences, 113 (16) 4296 4301; DOI: 10.1073/pnas1516047113. https://www.pnas.org/content/113/16/4296/tab-figures-data
10. Shealey, M. (2020, September 21). Overcoming Racial Battle Fatigue Through Education Reform [web log]. https://edprepmatters.net/2020/09/overcoming-racial-battle-fatigue-through-education-reform/.
11. Frost, R. "Stopping by Woods on a Snowy Evening." *Collected Poems, Prose, & Plays*. Library of America.

Chapter Eleven

1. Arians, NFL Prime Time, 2021.

HOSEA 4:6

www.ingramcontent.com/pod-product-compliance
Lightning Source LLC
Chambersburg PA
CBHW071826080526
44589CB00012B/928